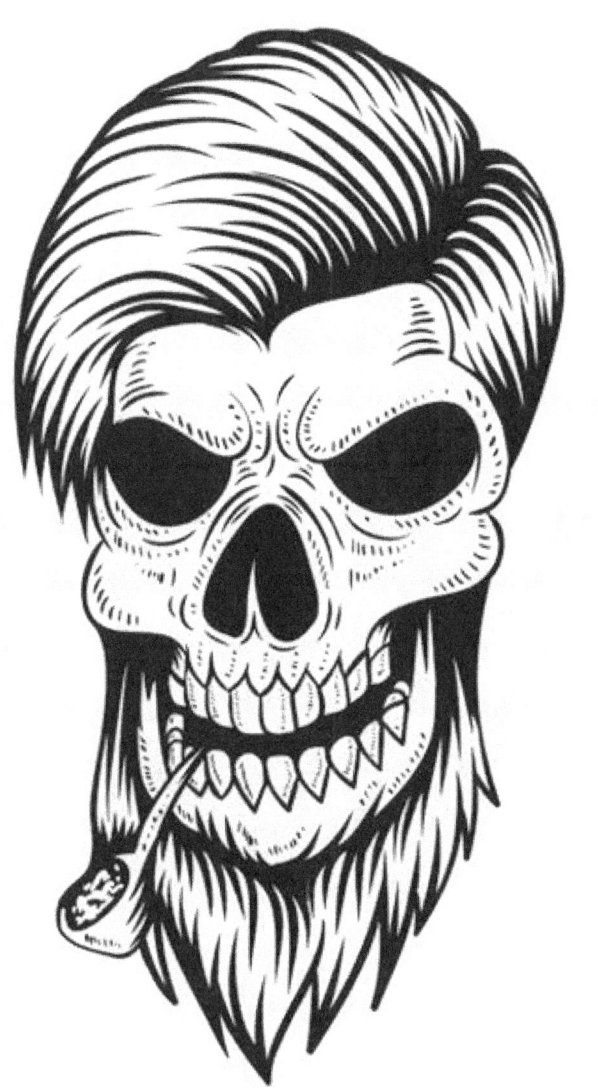

# THIS BOOK BELONG TO

-------------------------------

-------------------------------

-------------------------------

# TEST COLOR

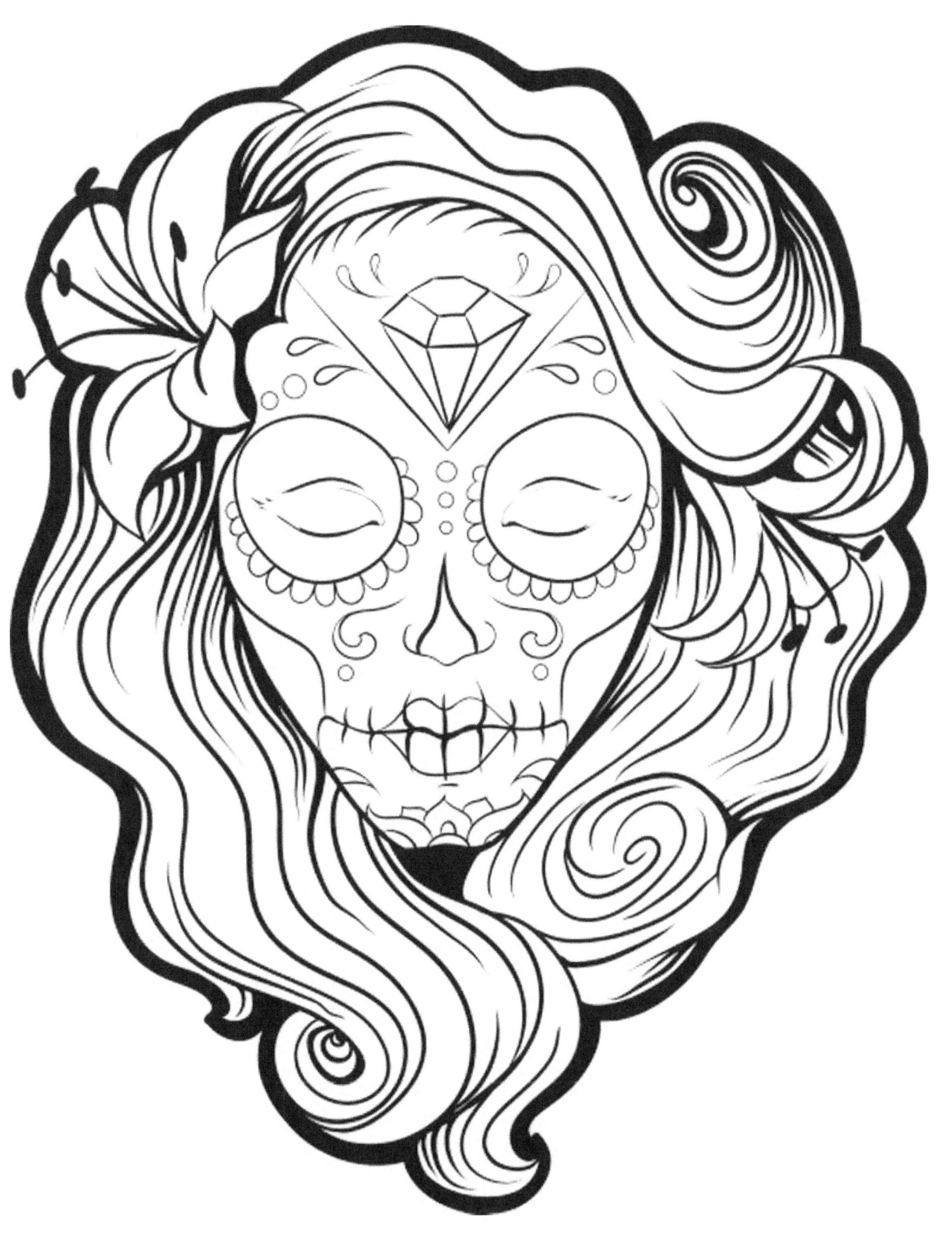

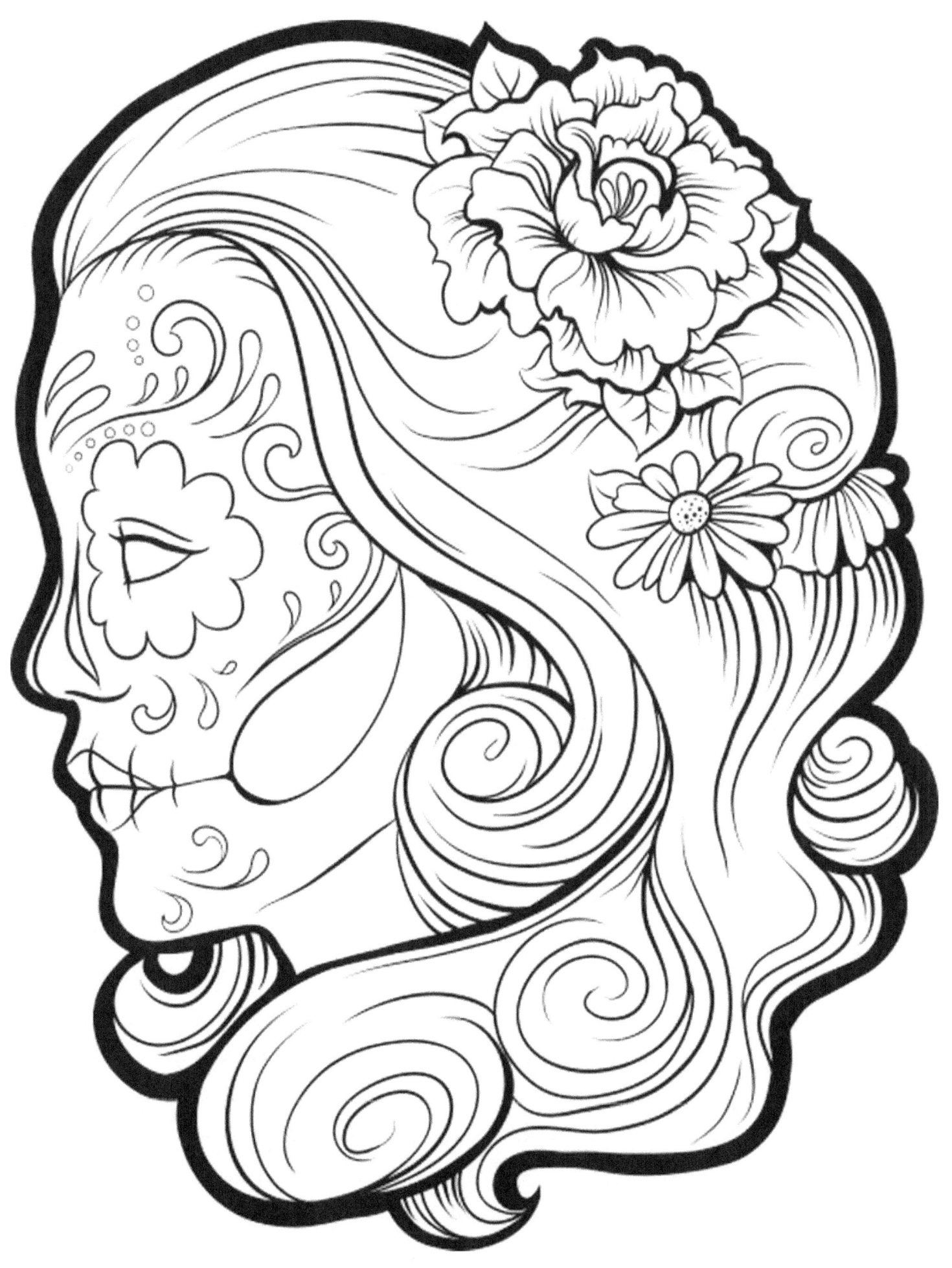

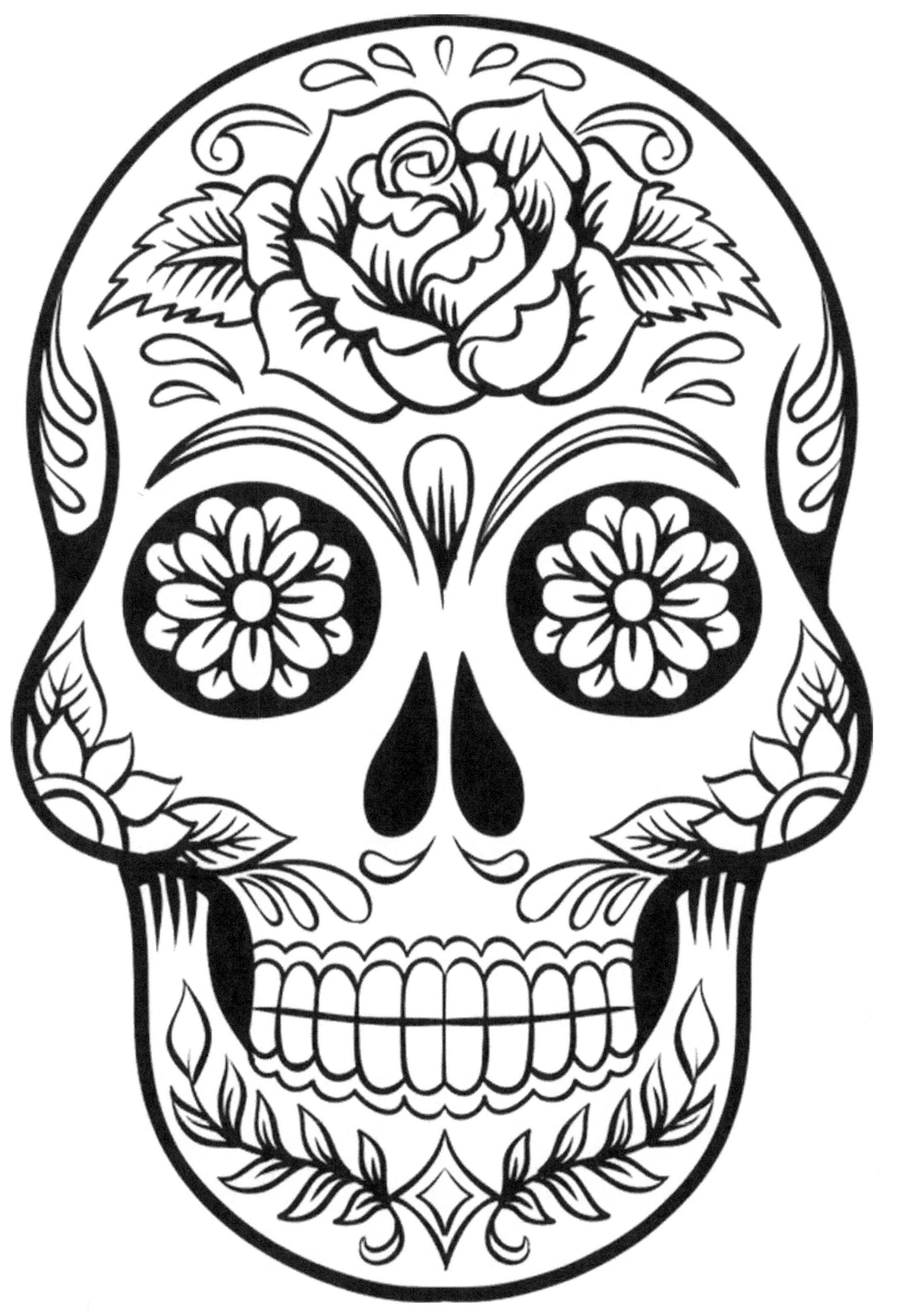

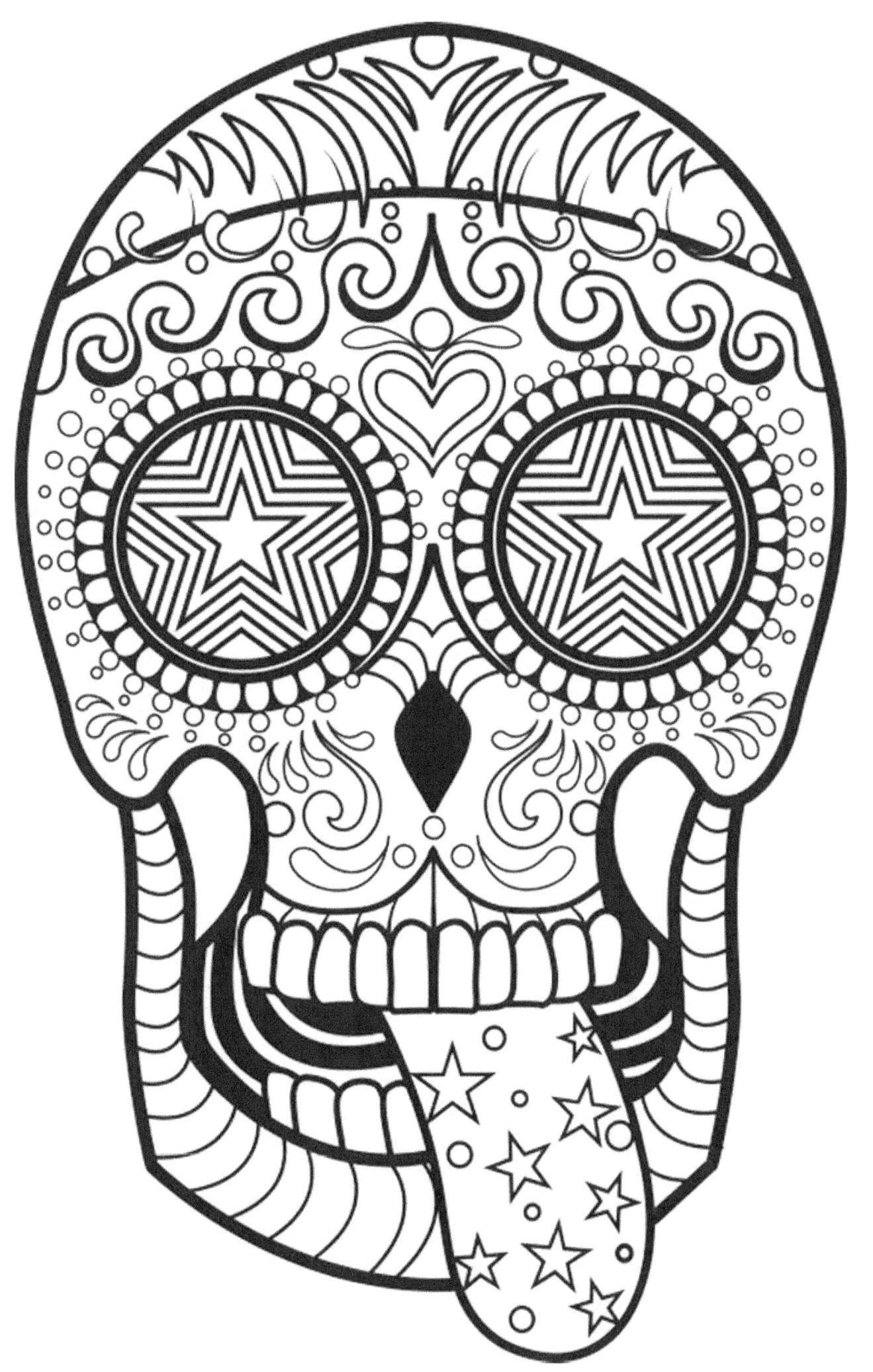

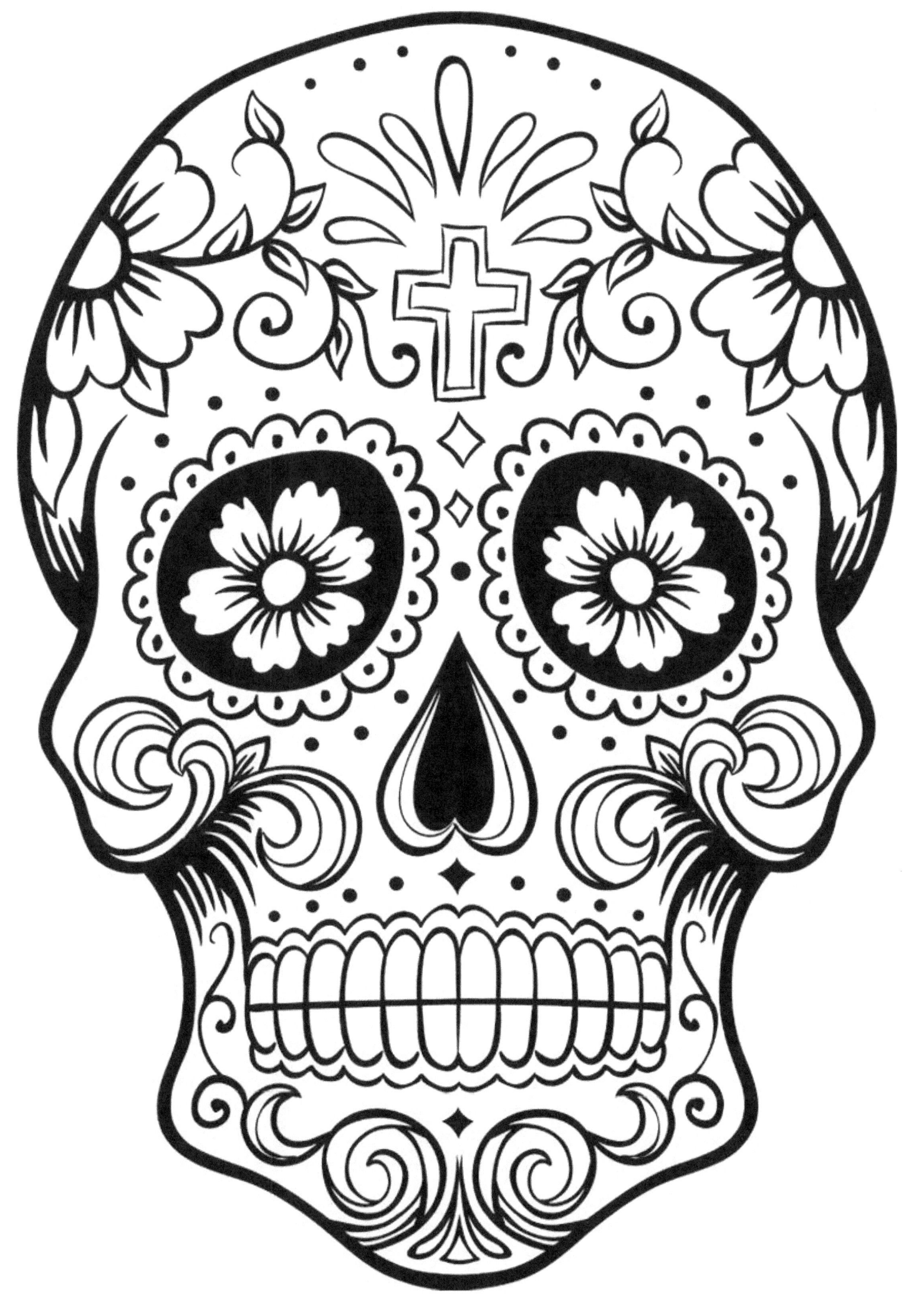

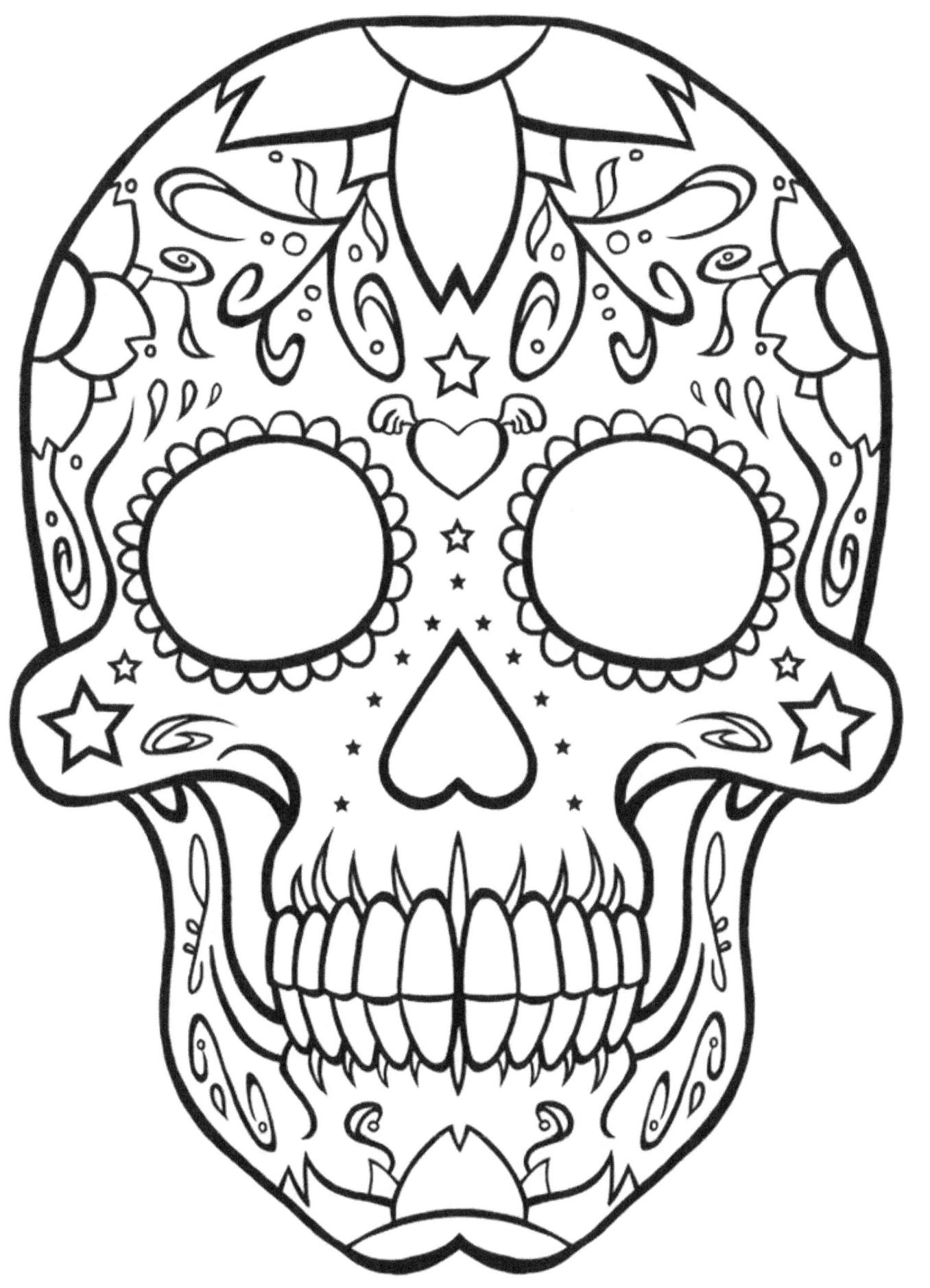

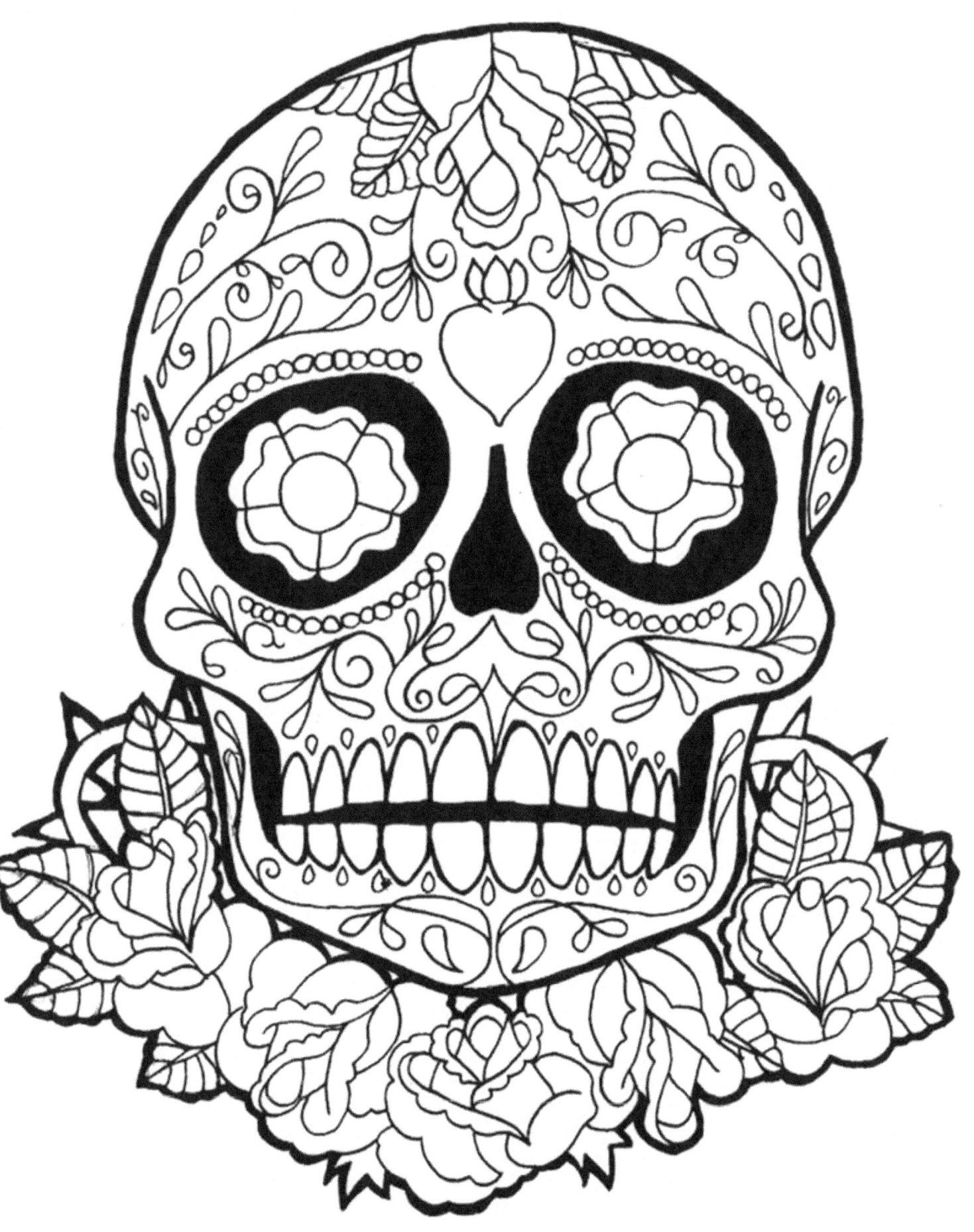

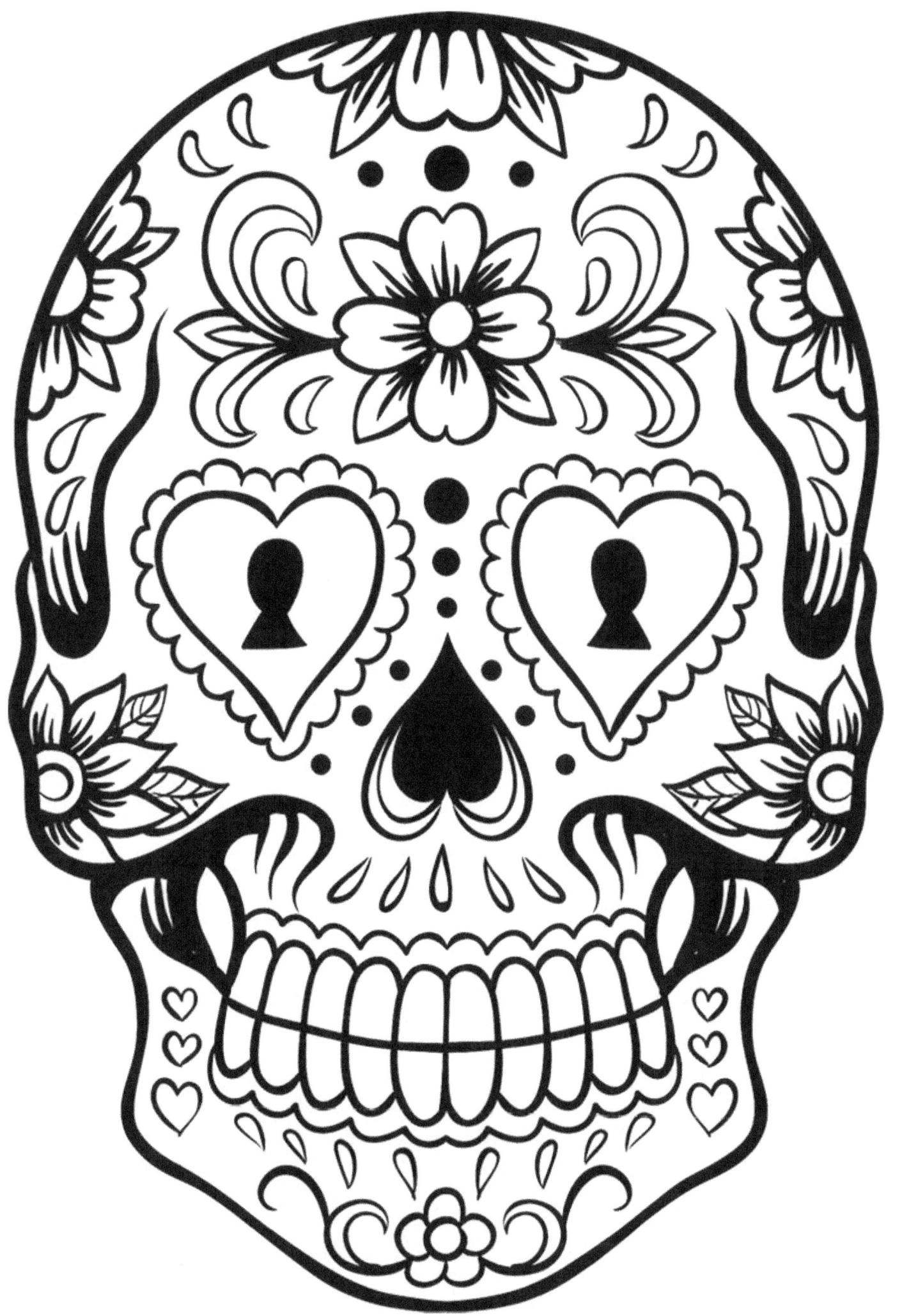

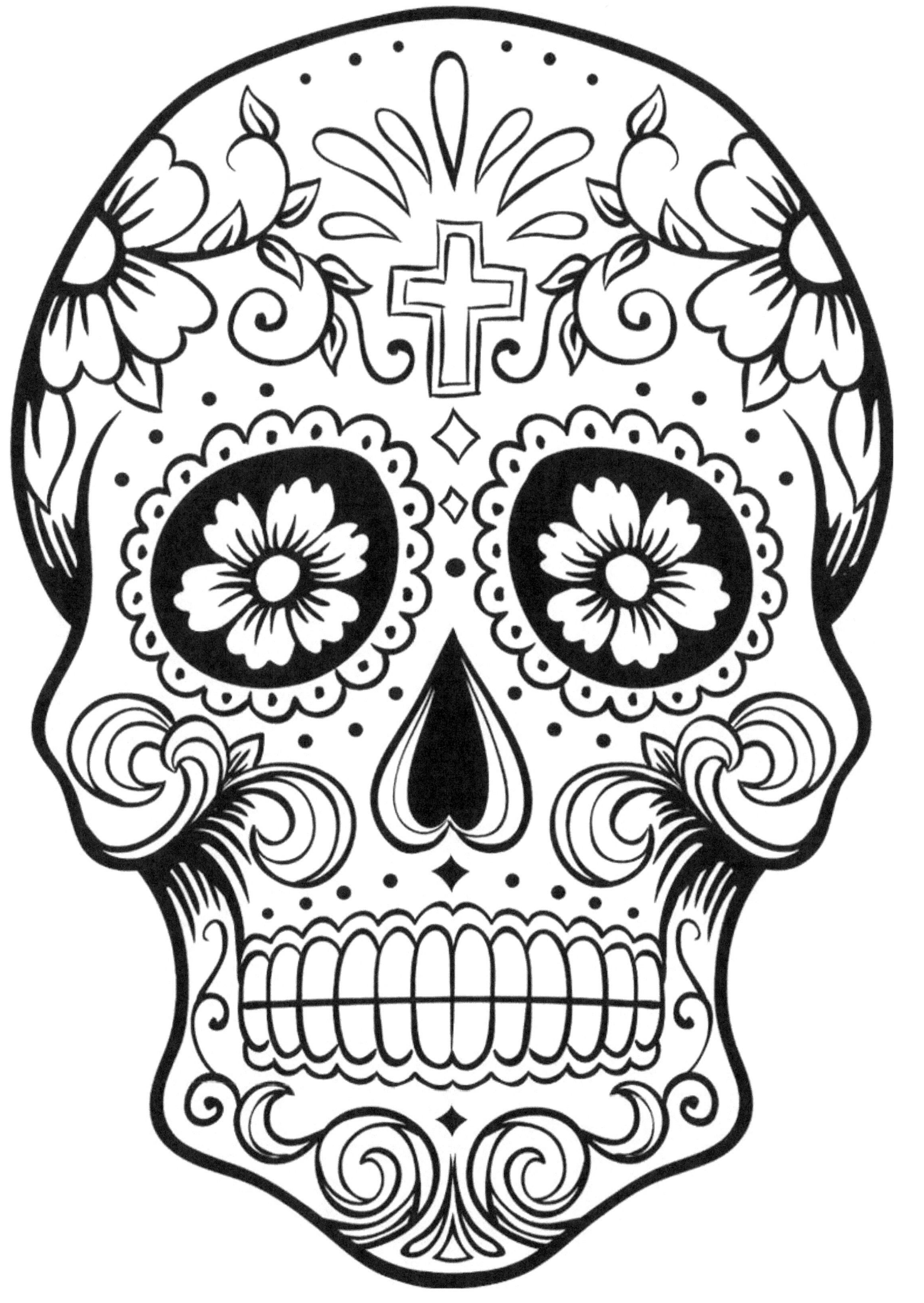

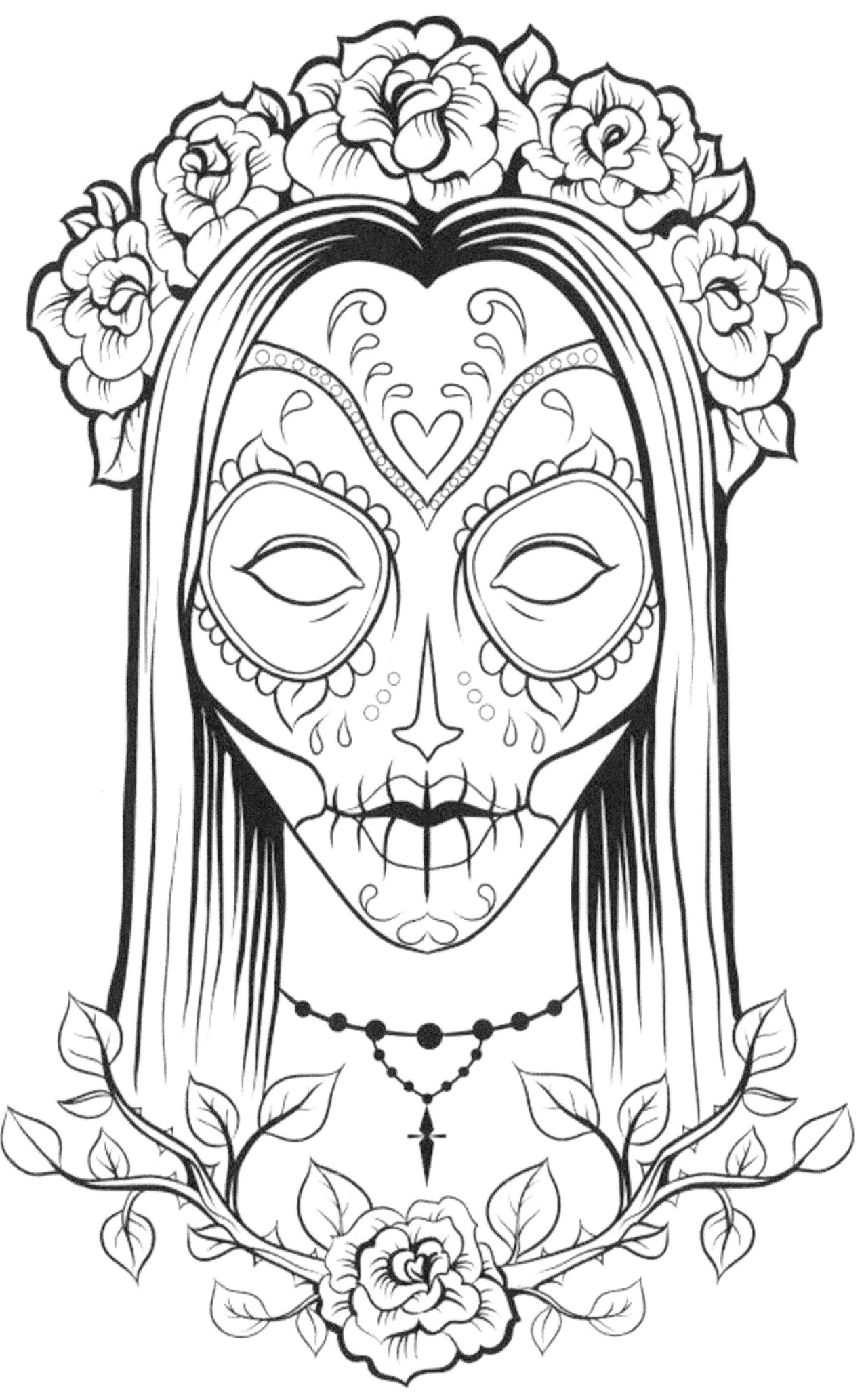

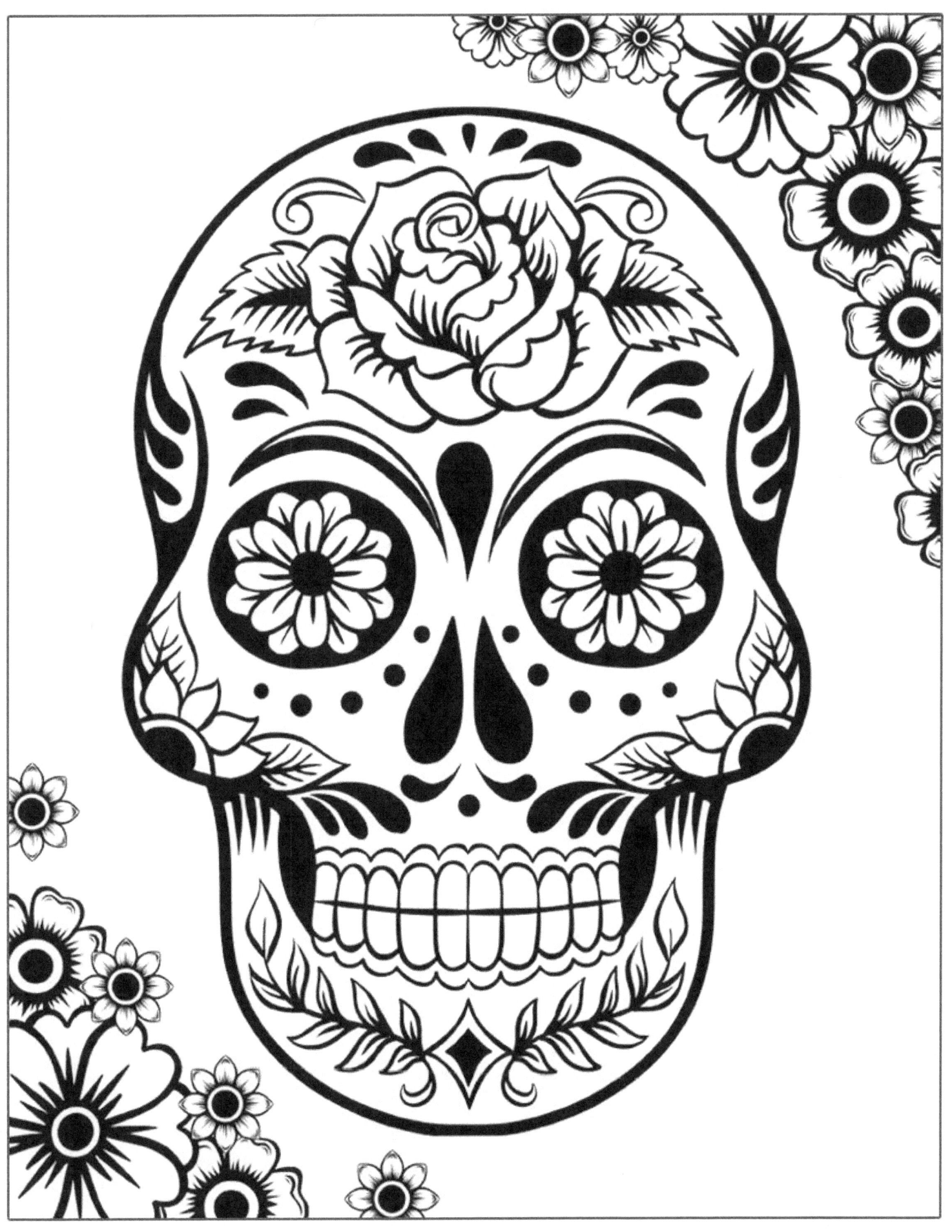

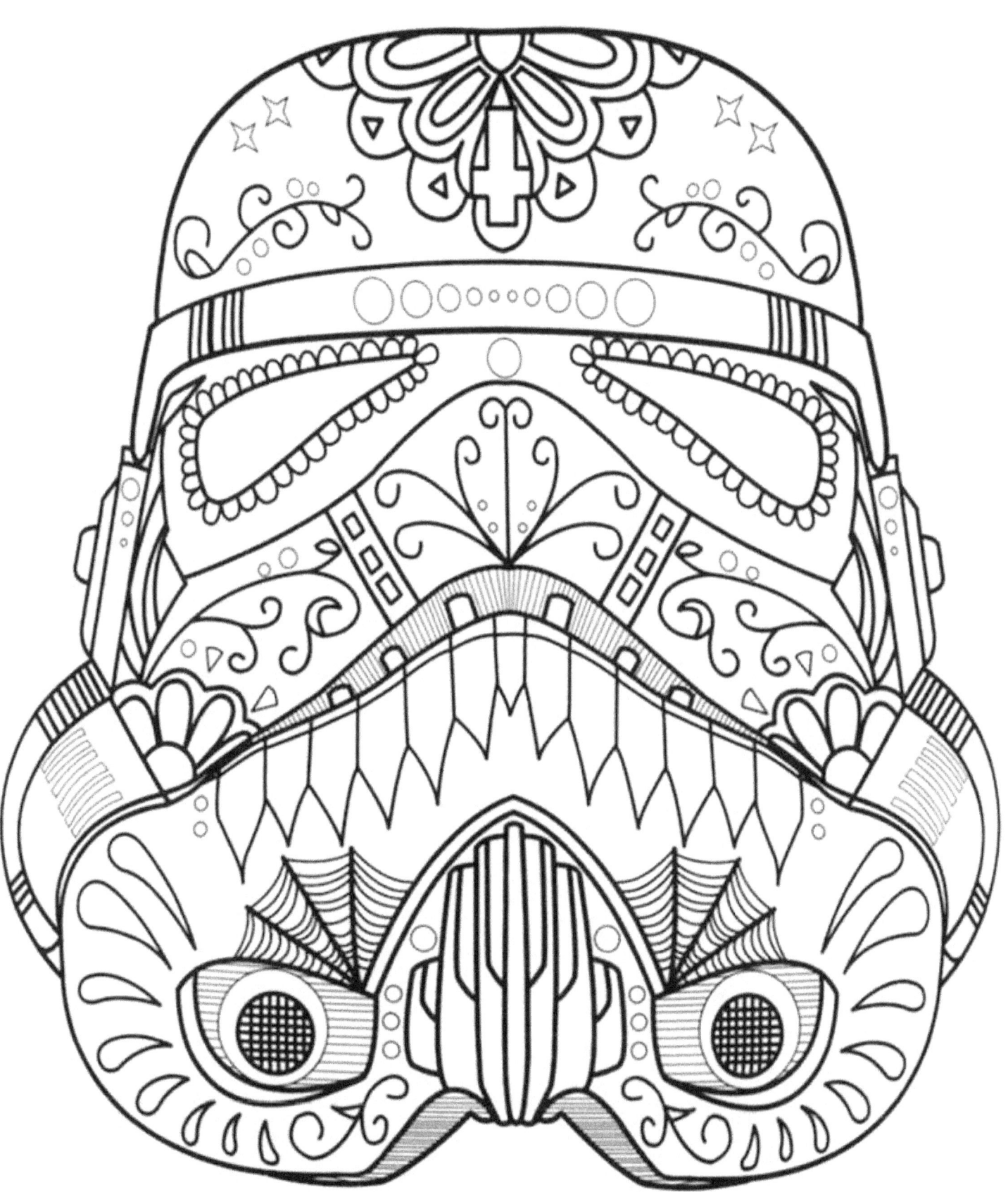

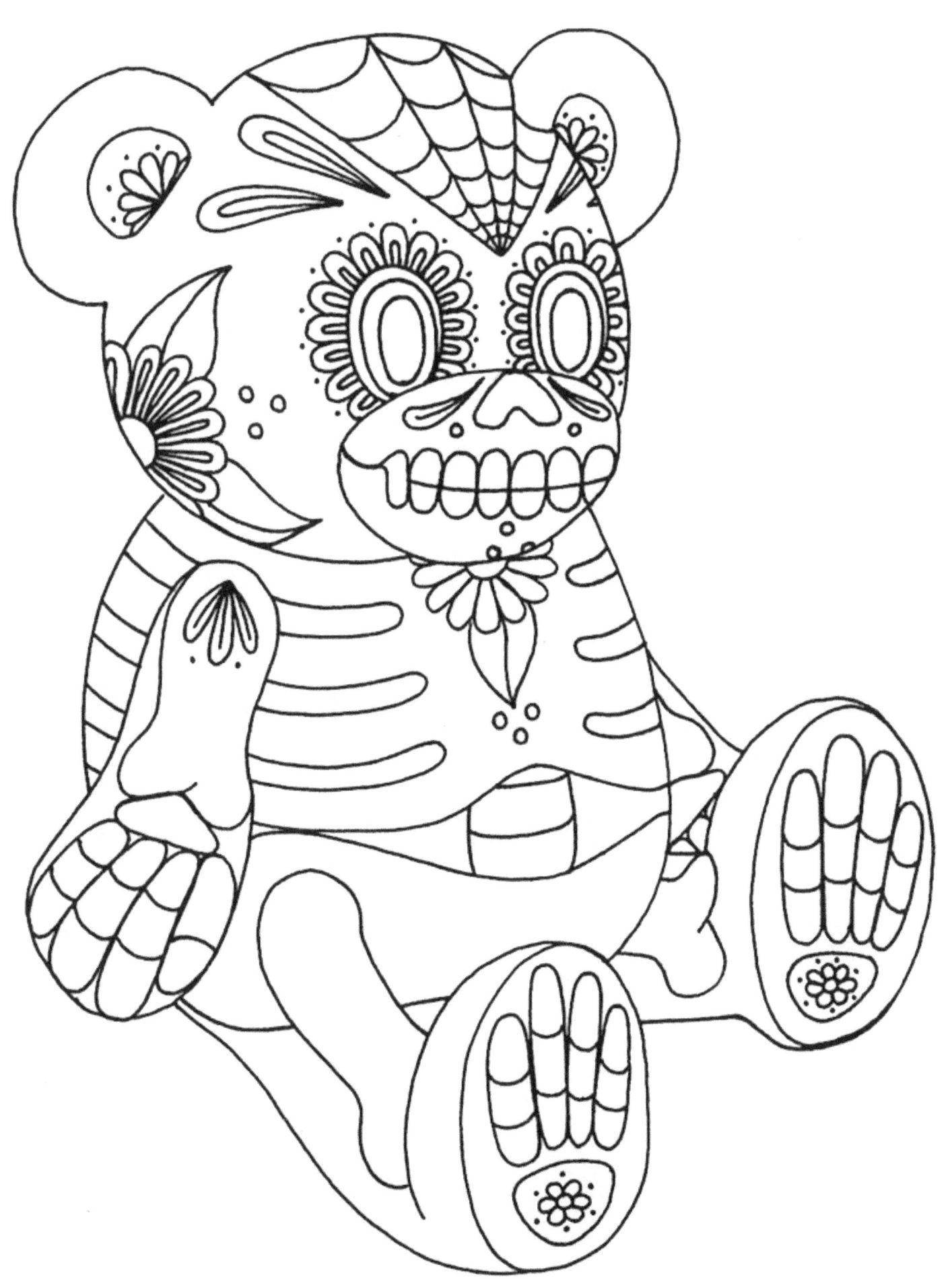

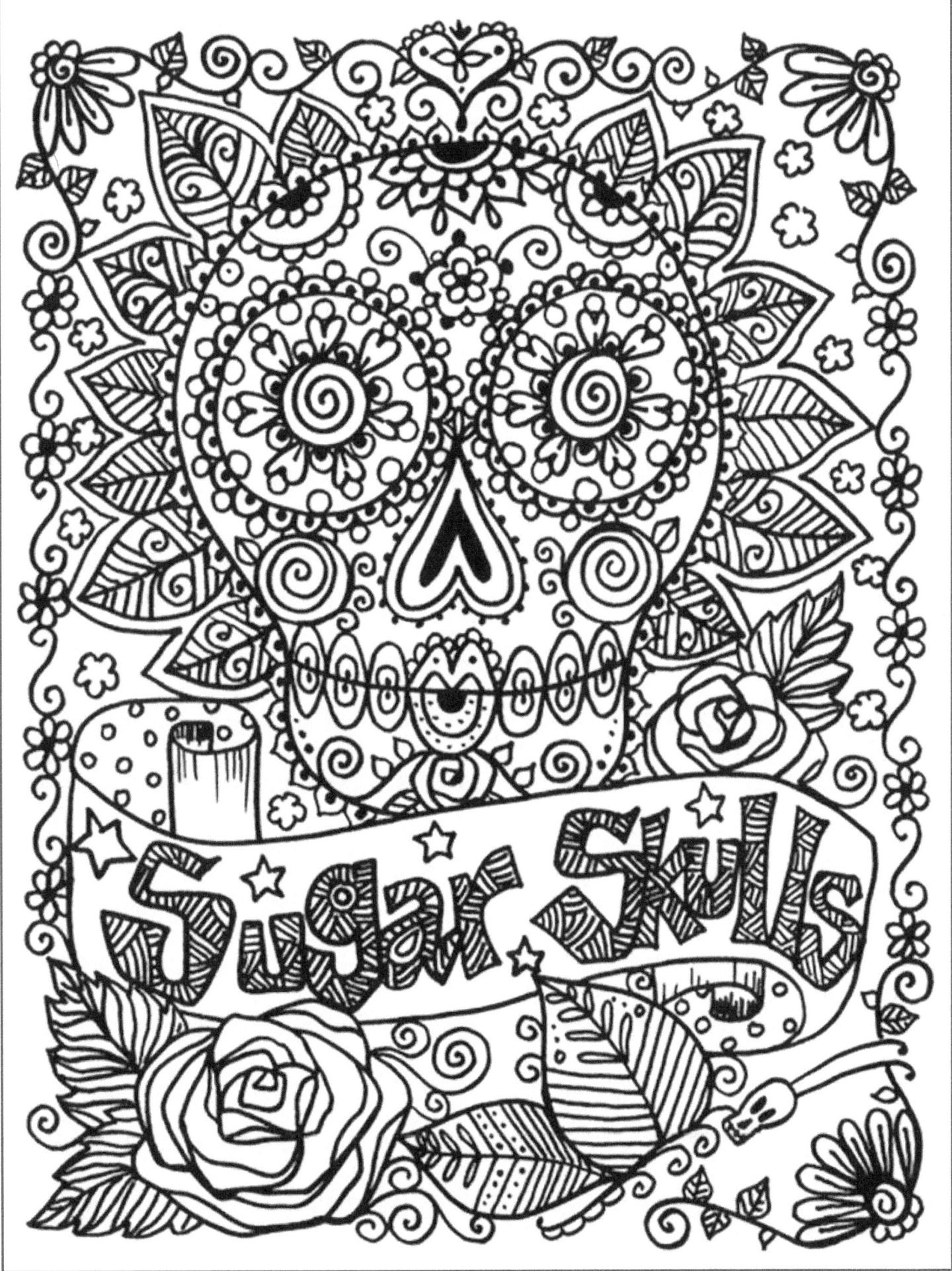

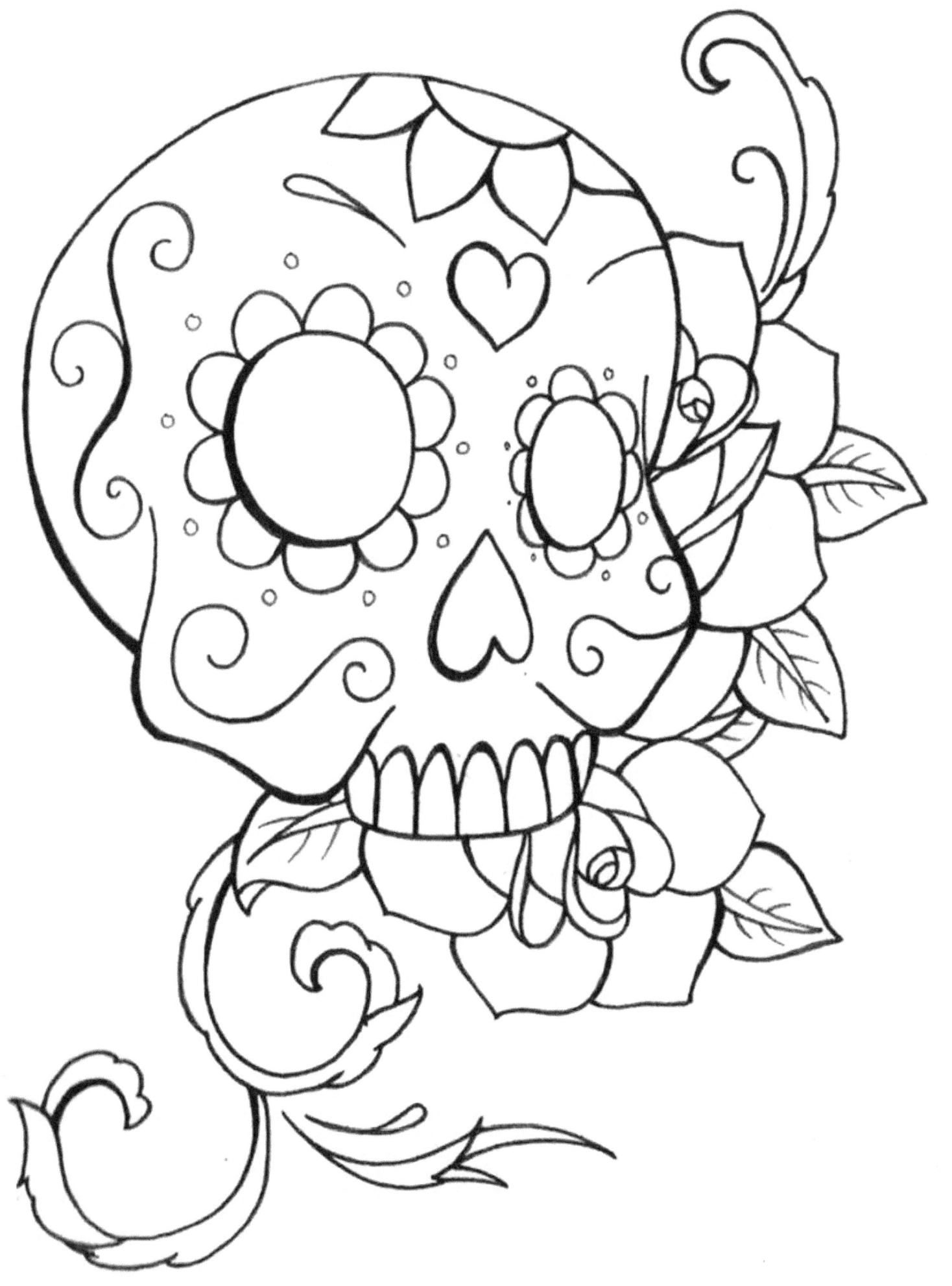

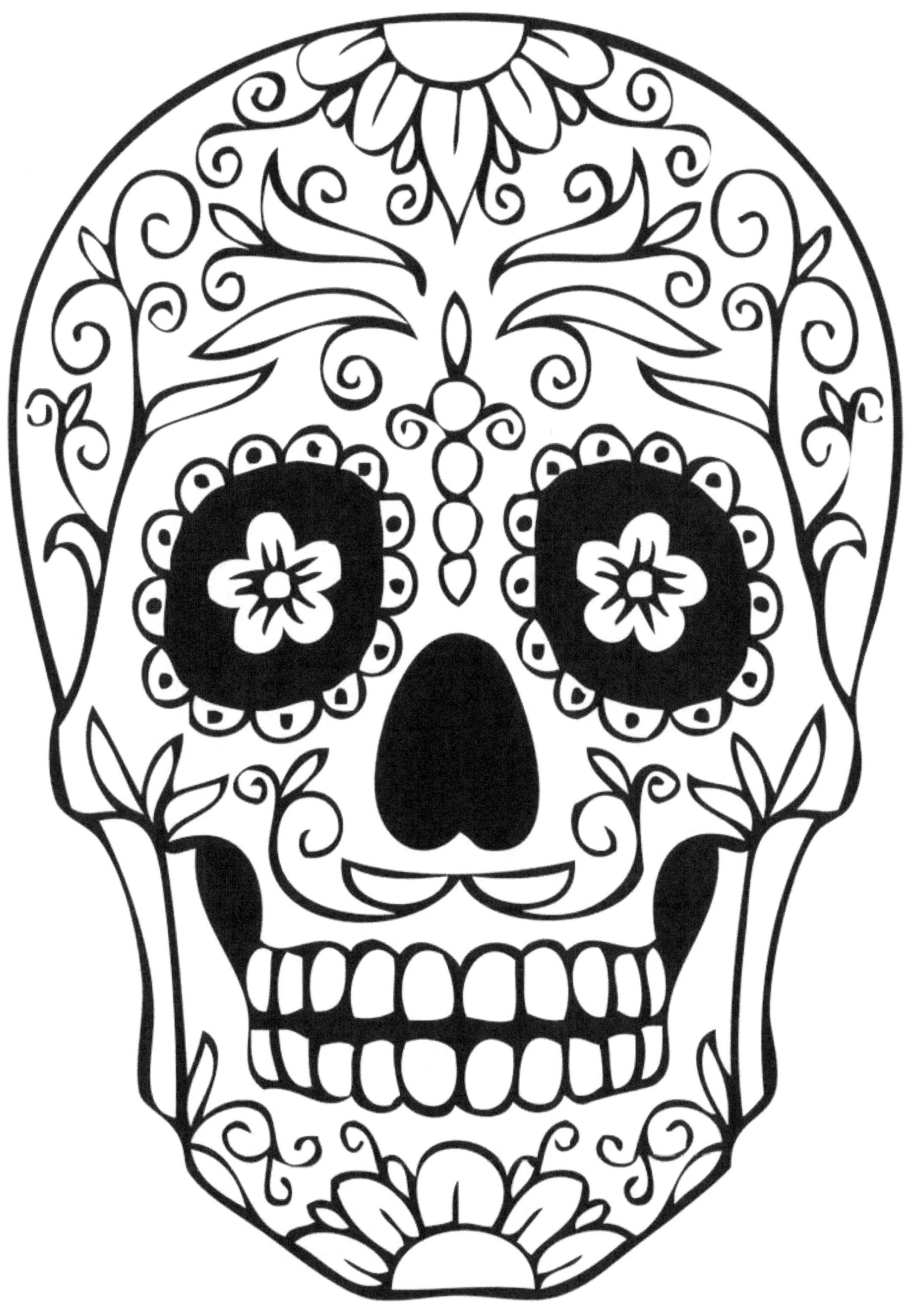

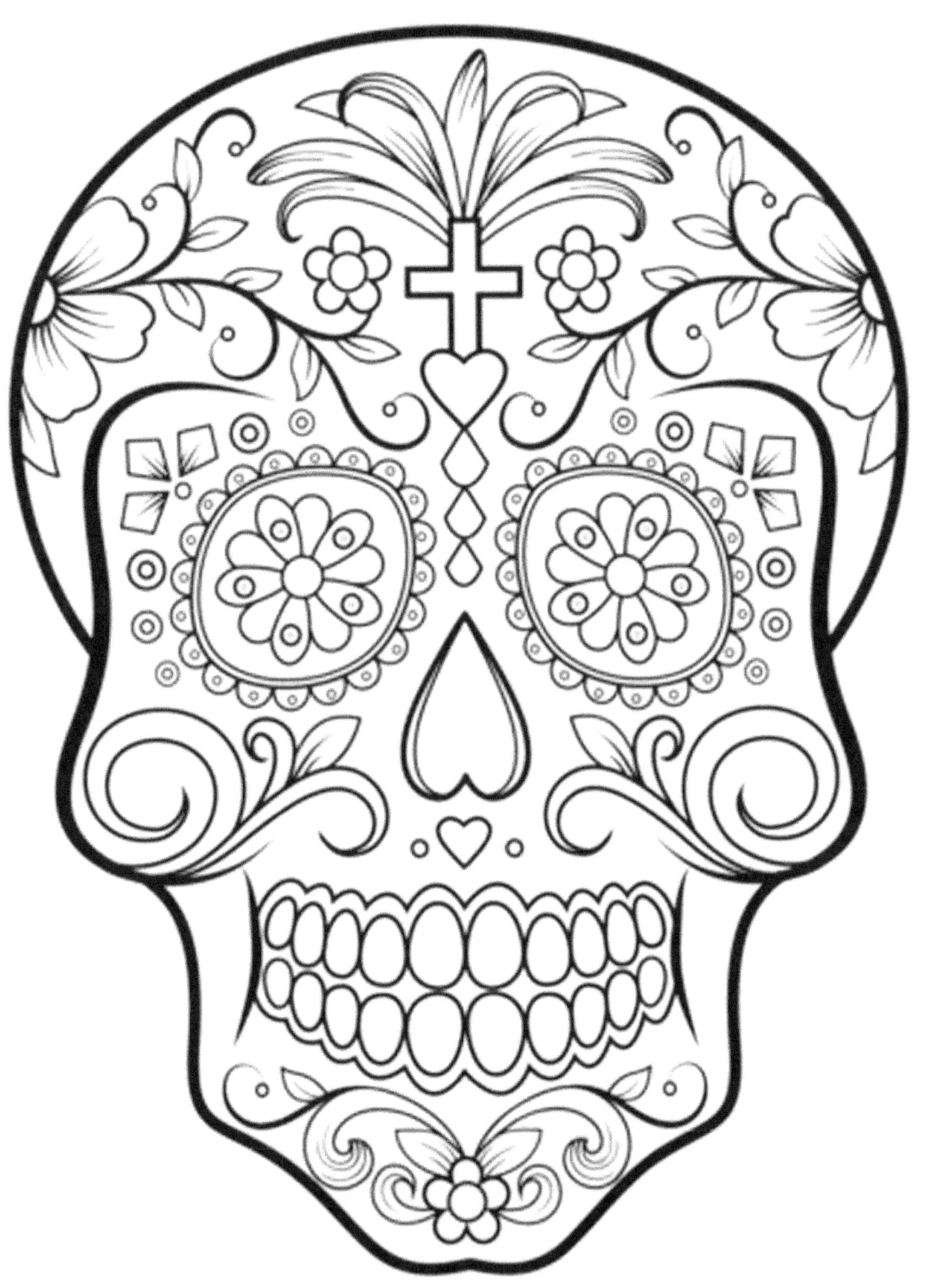

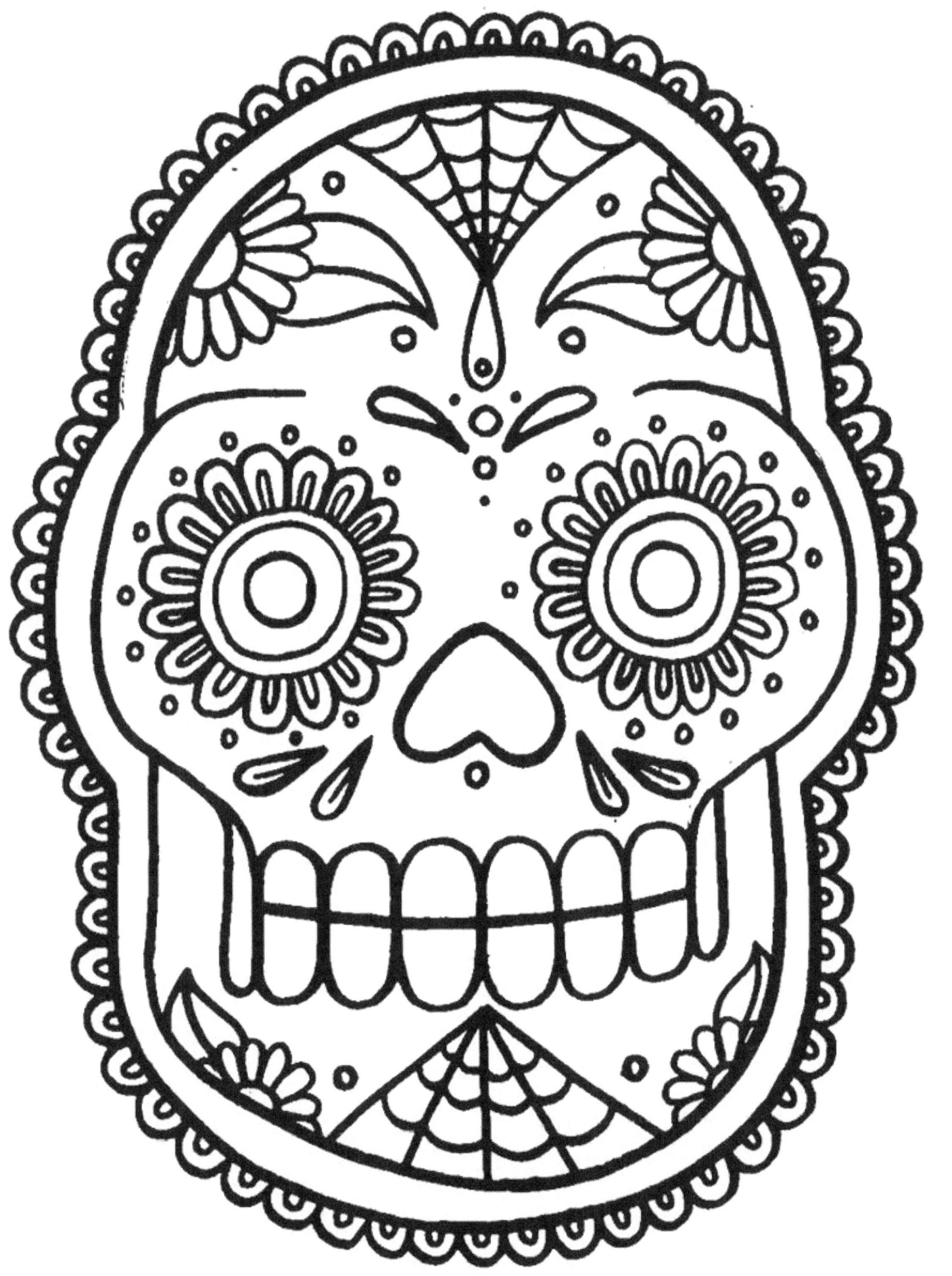

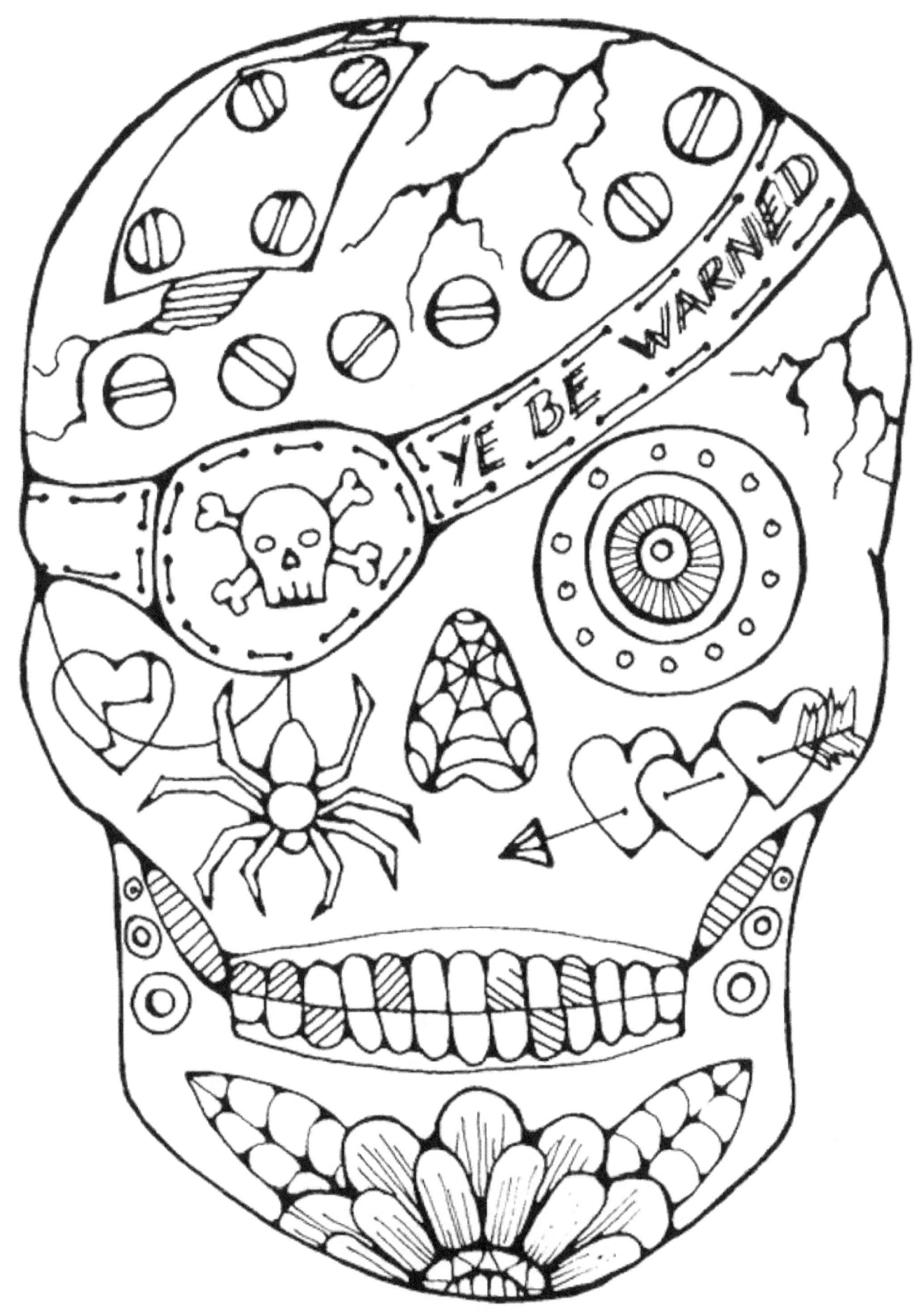

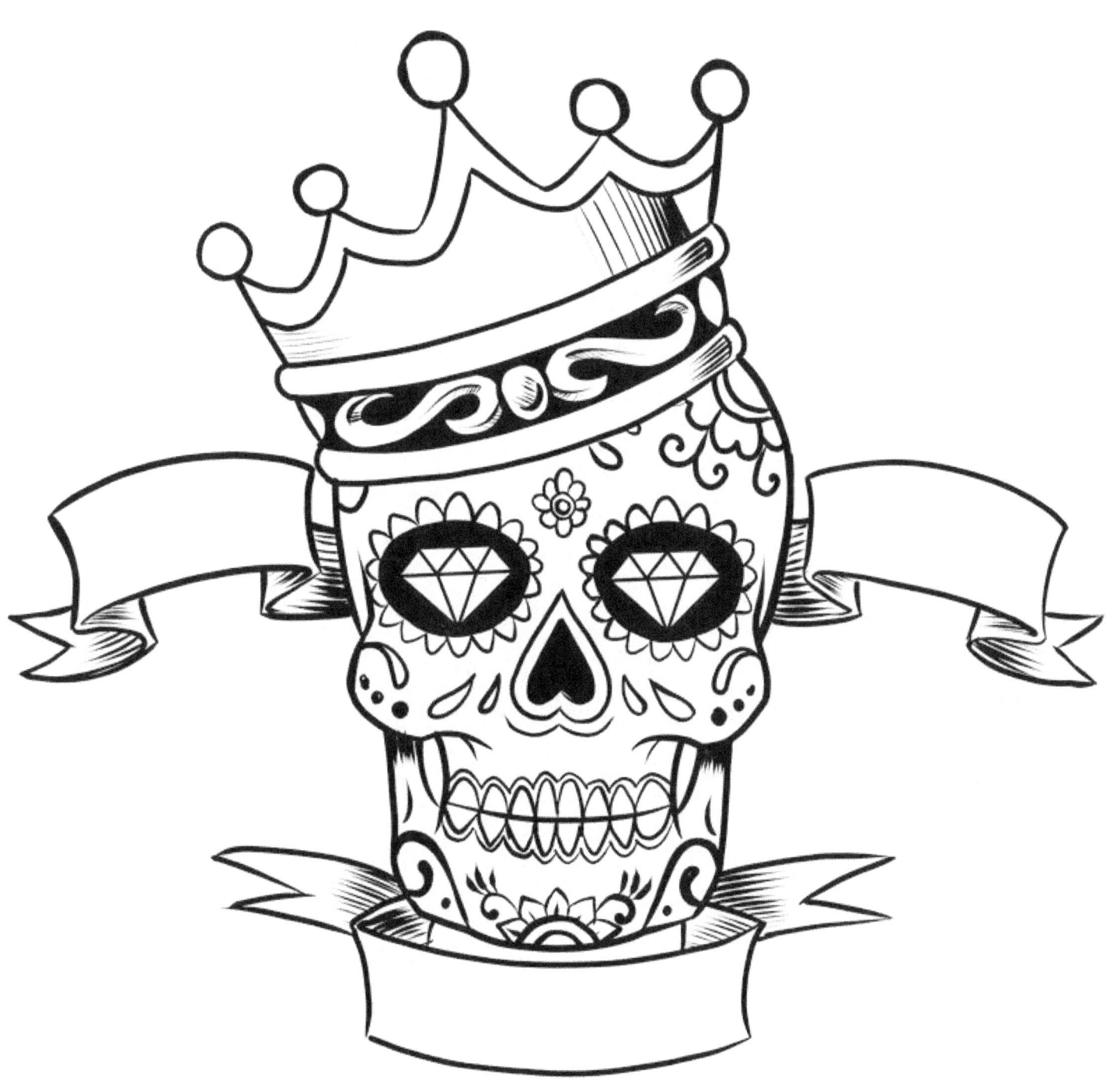

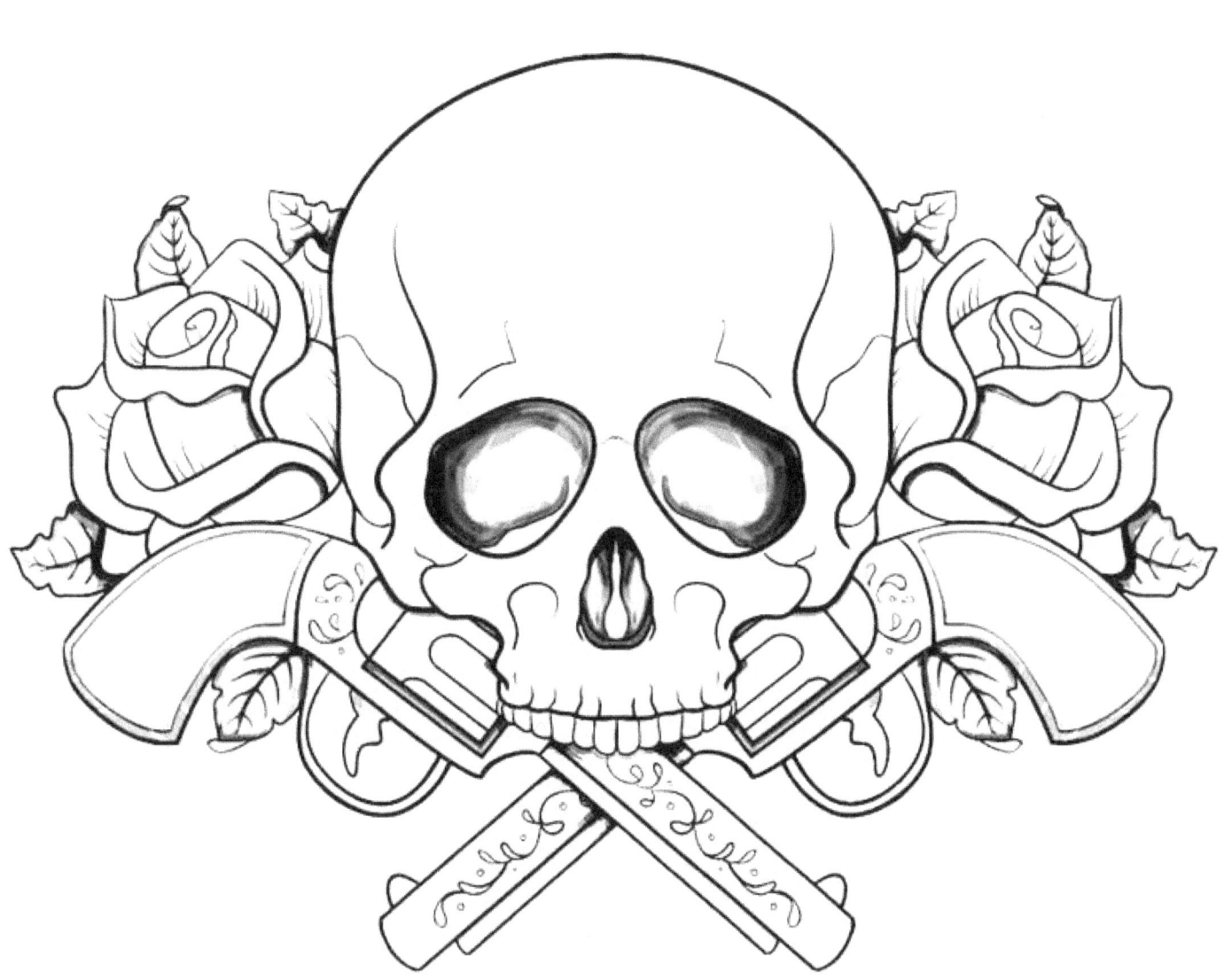

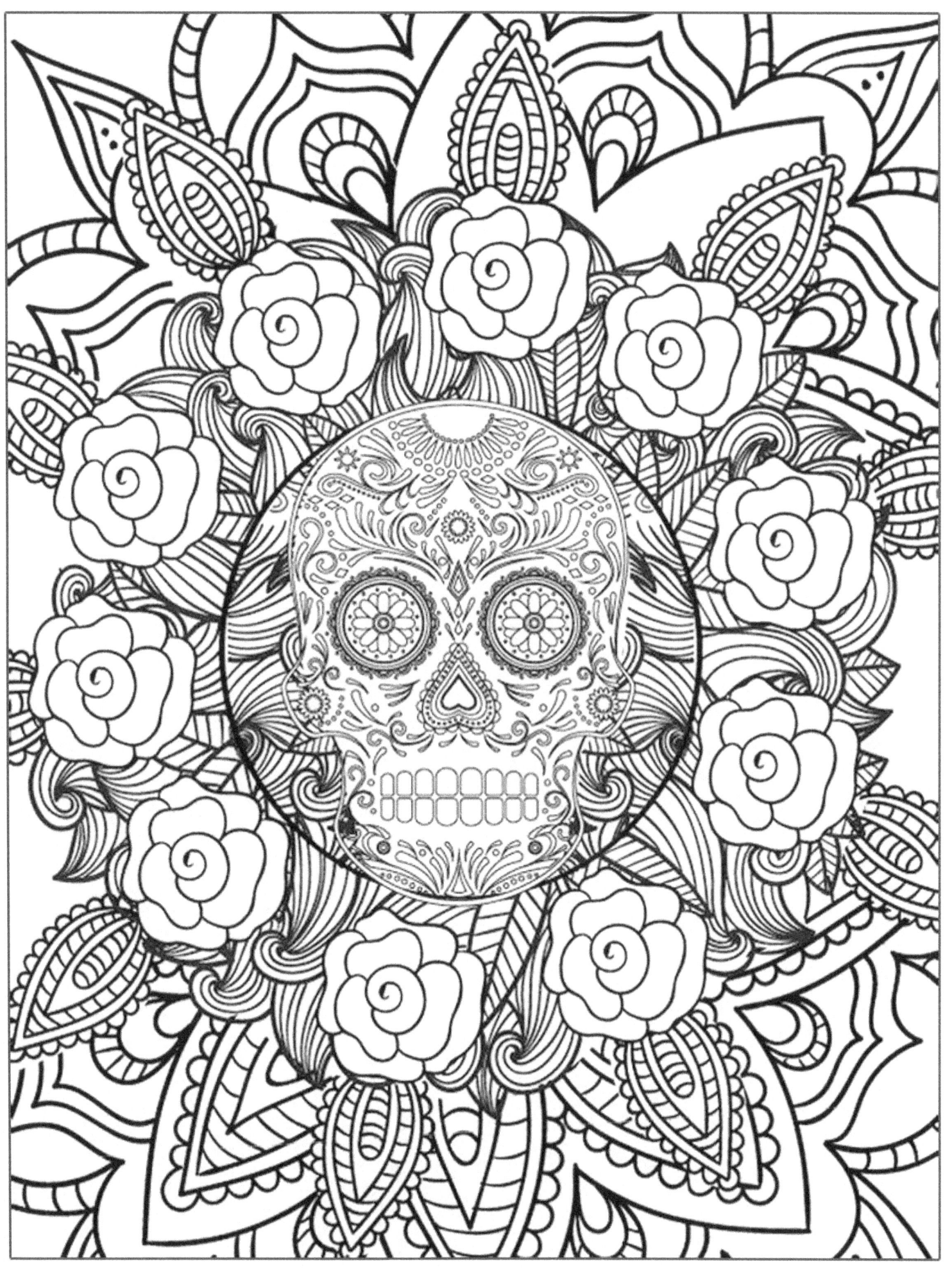

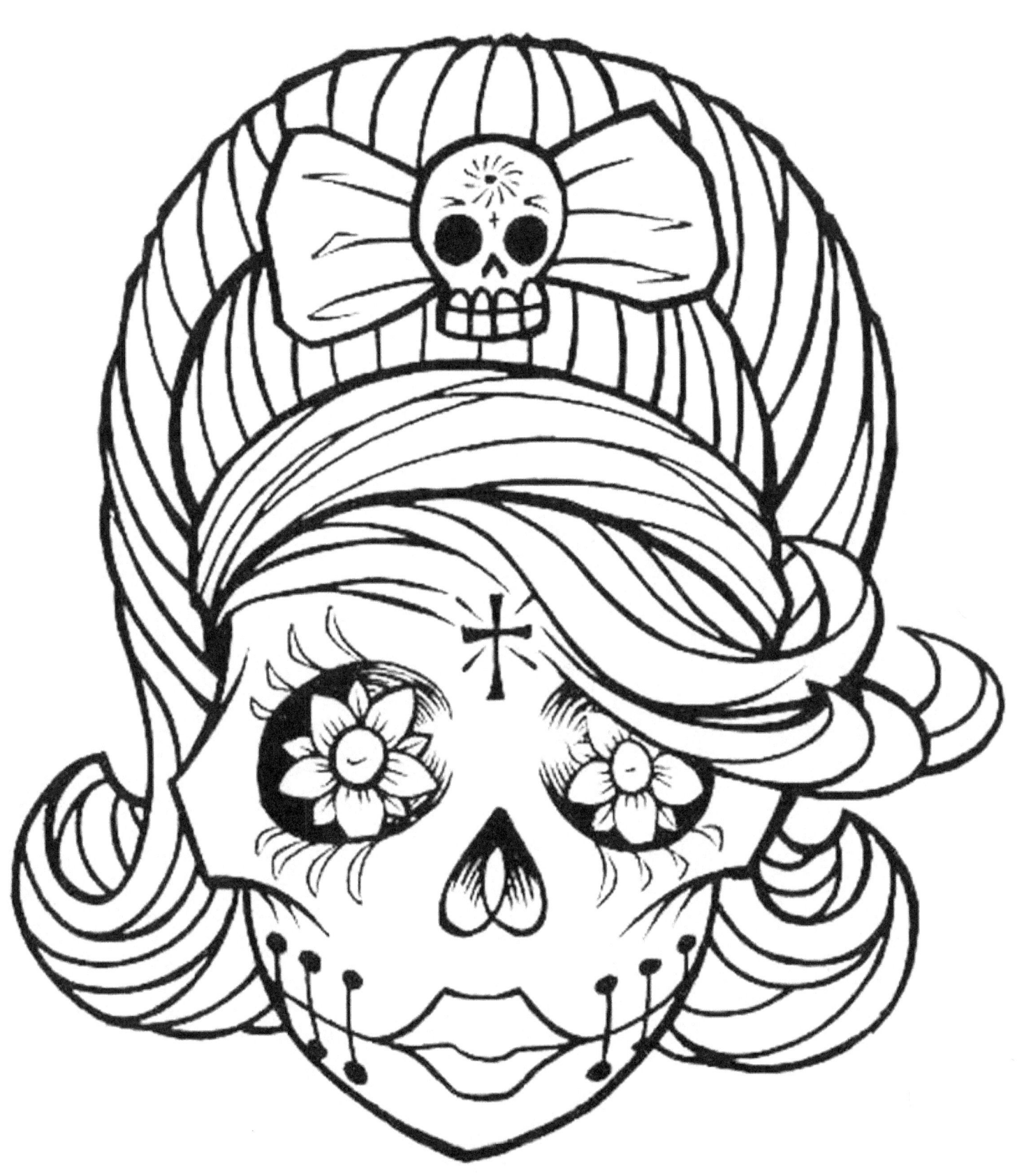

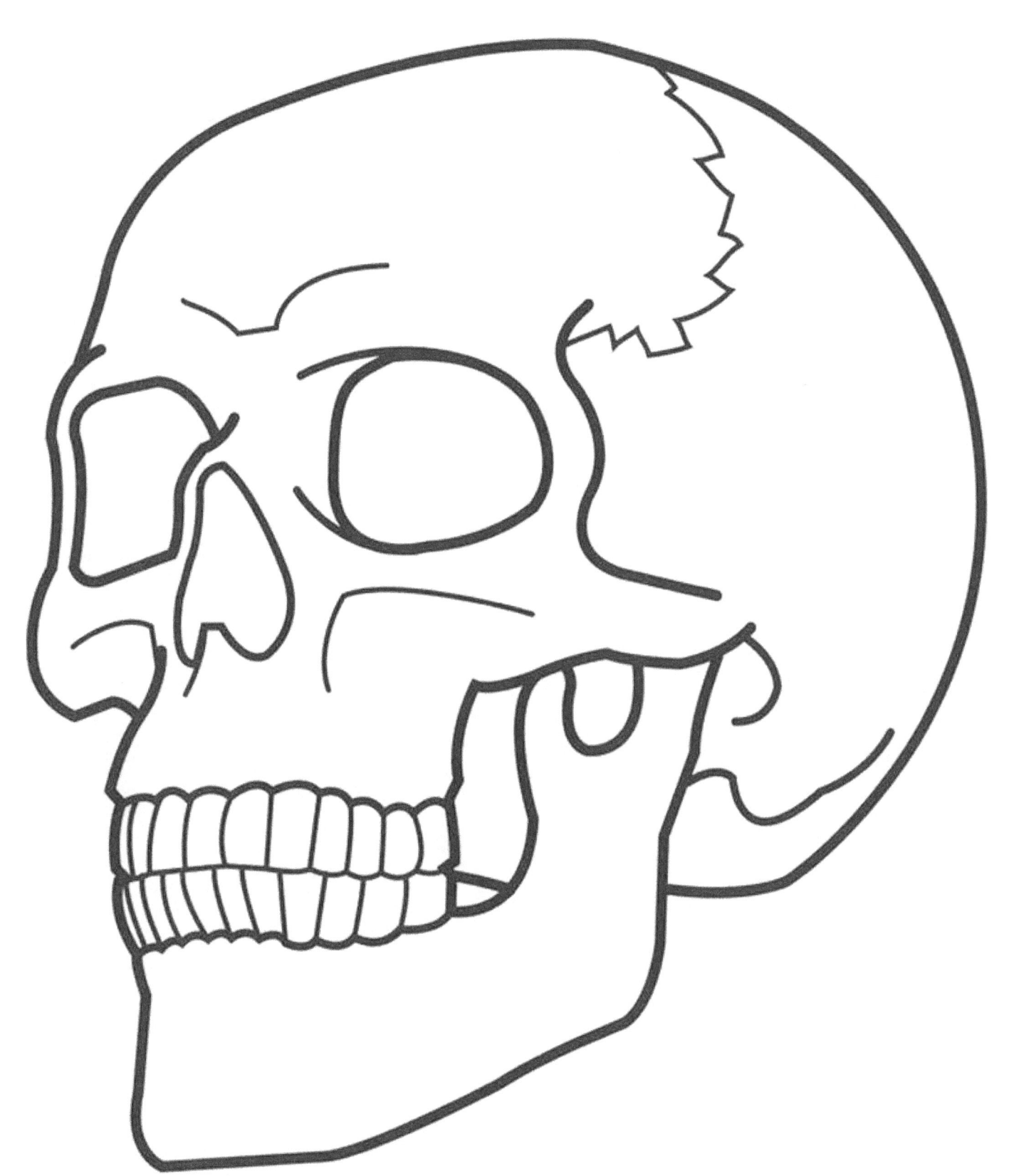

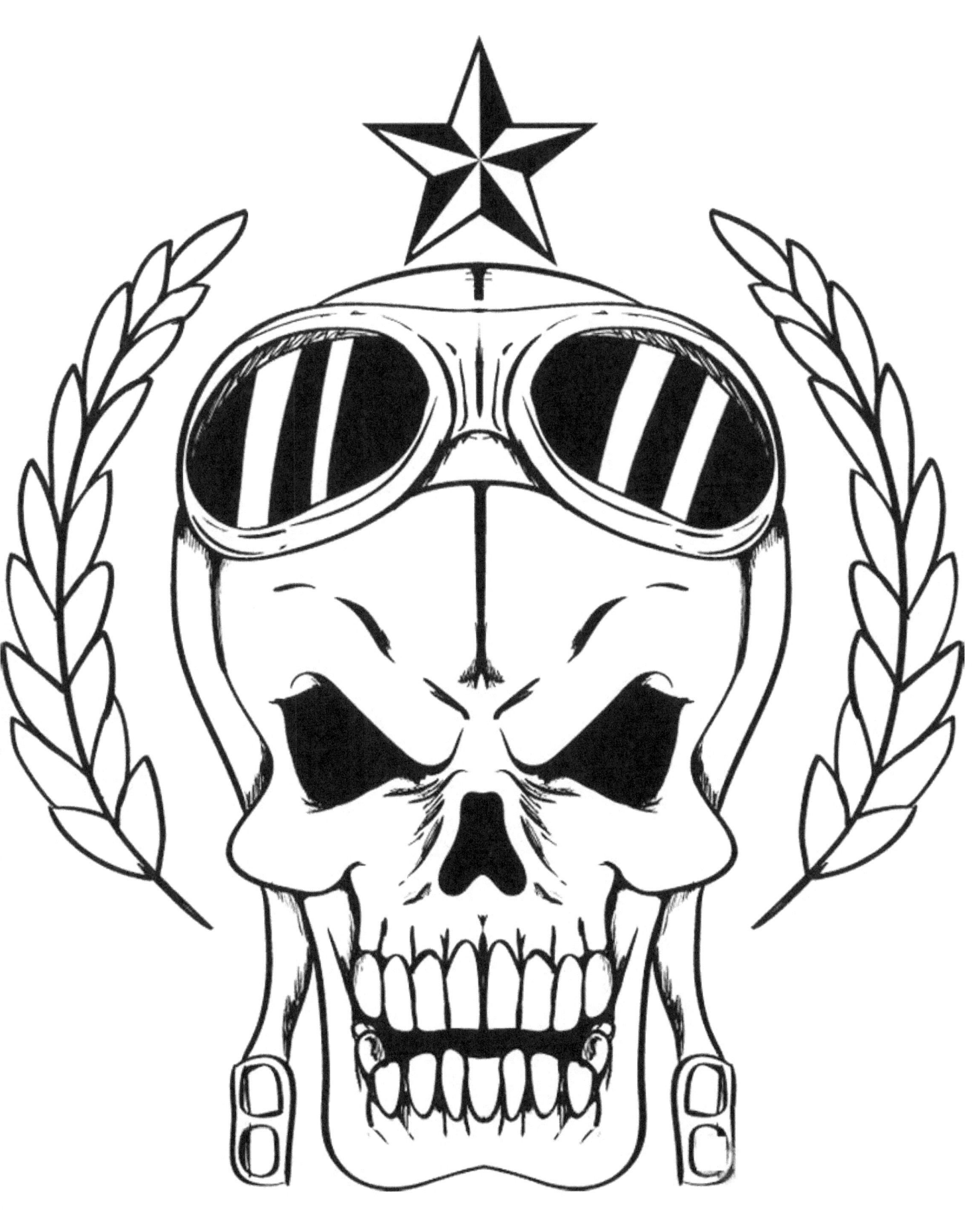

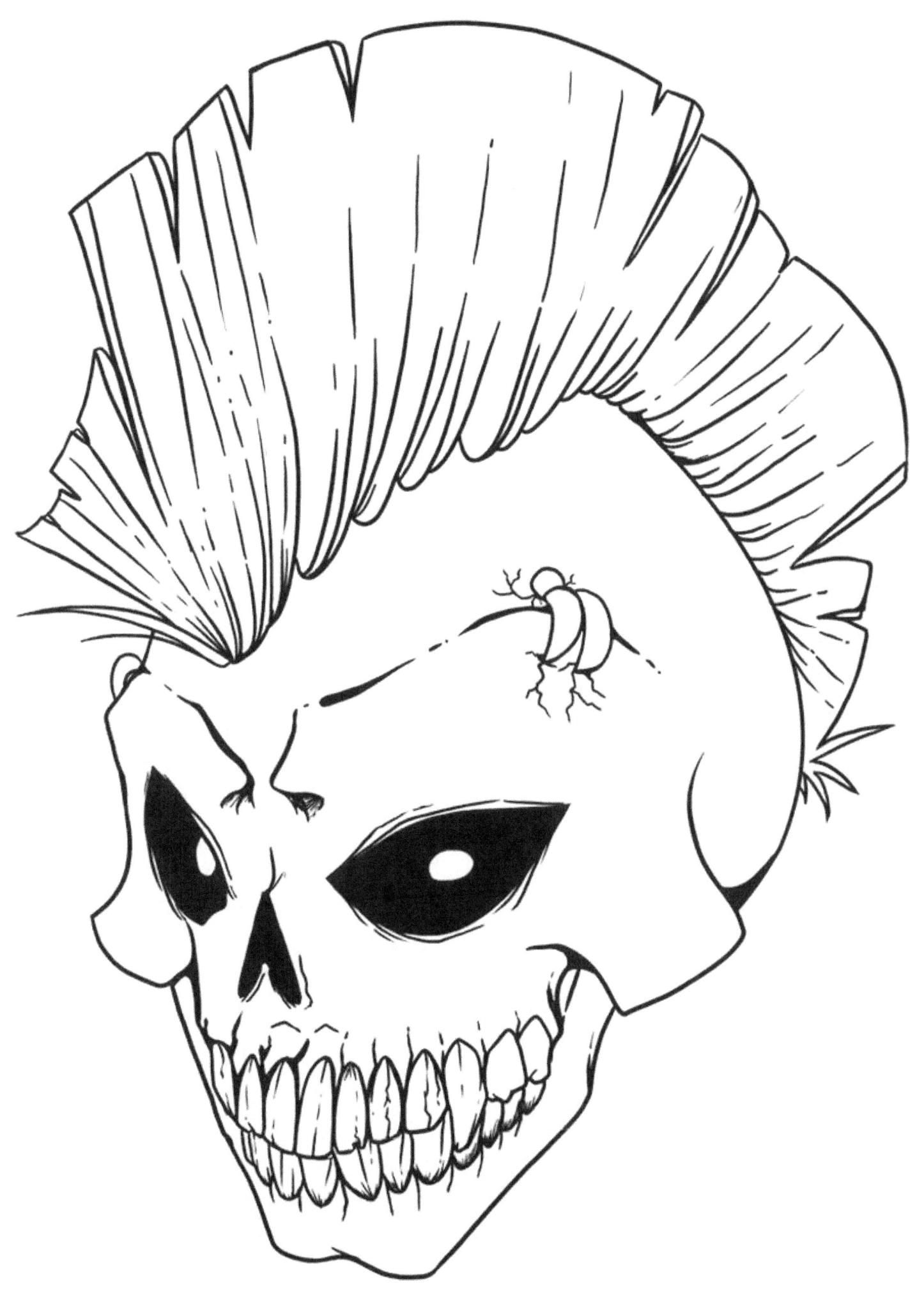

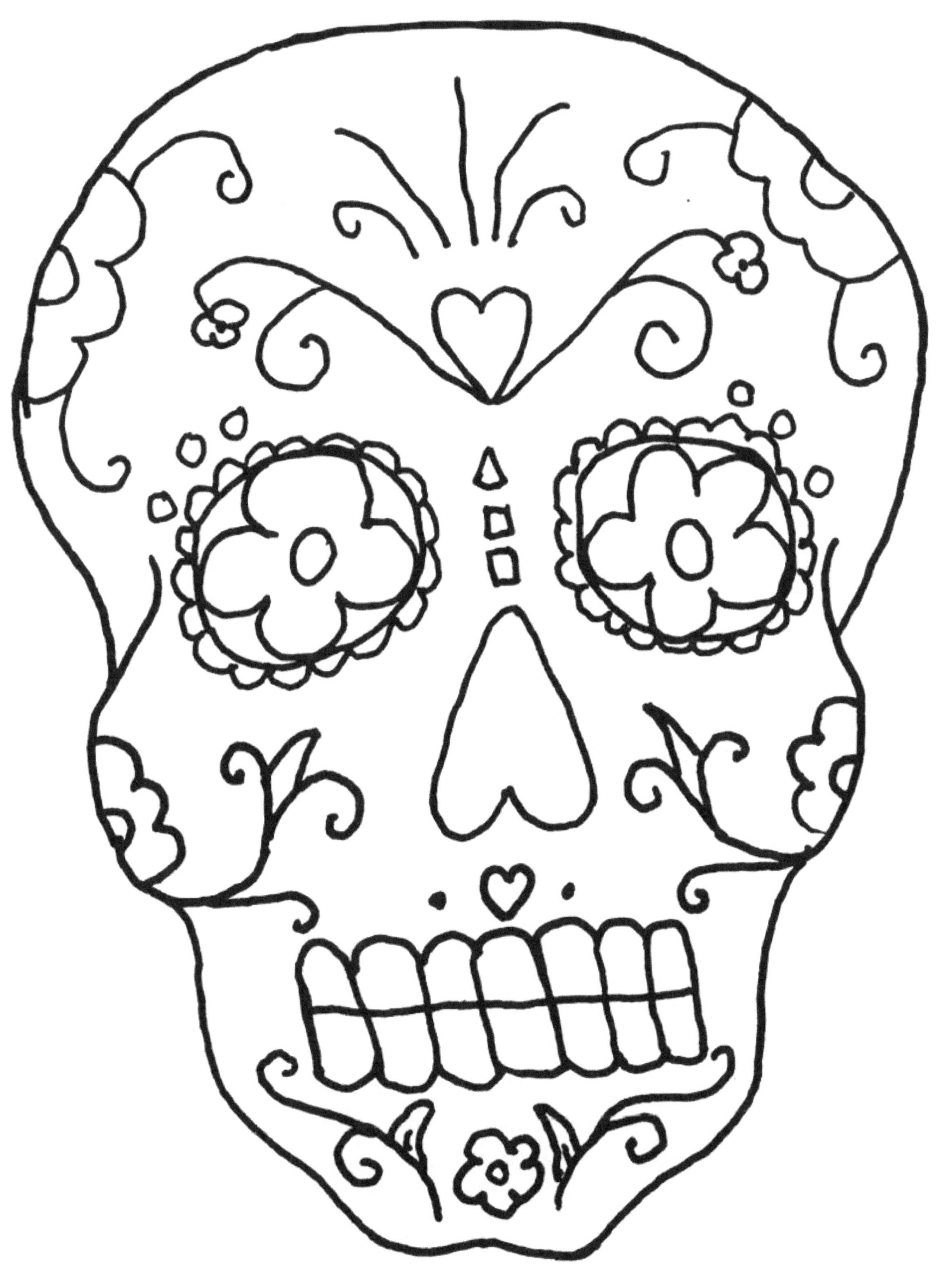

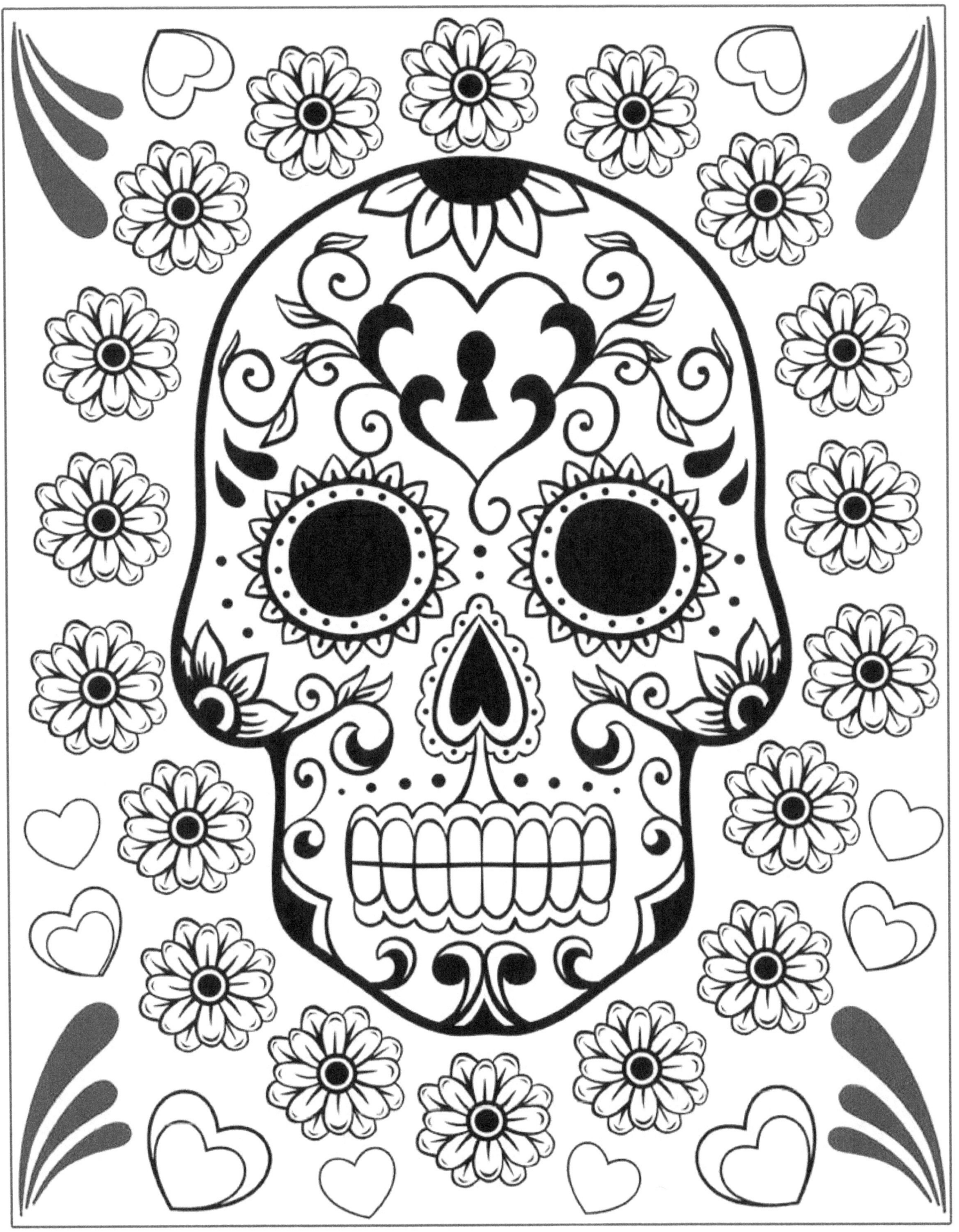

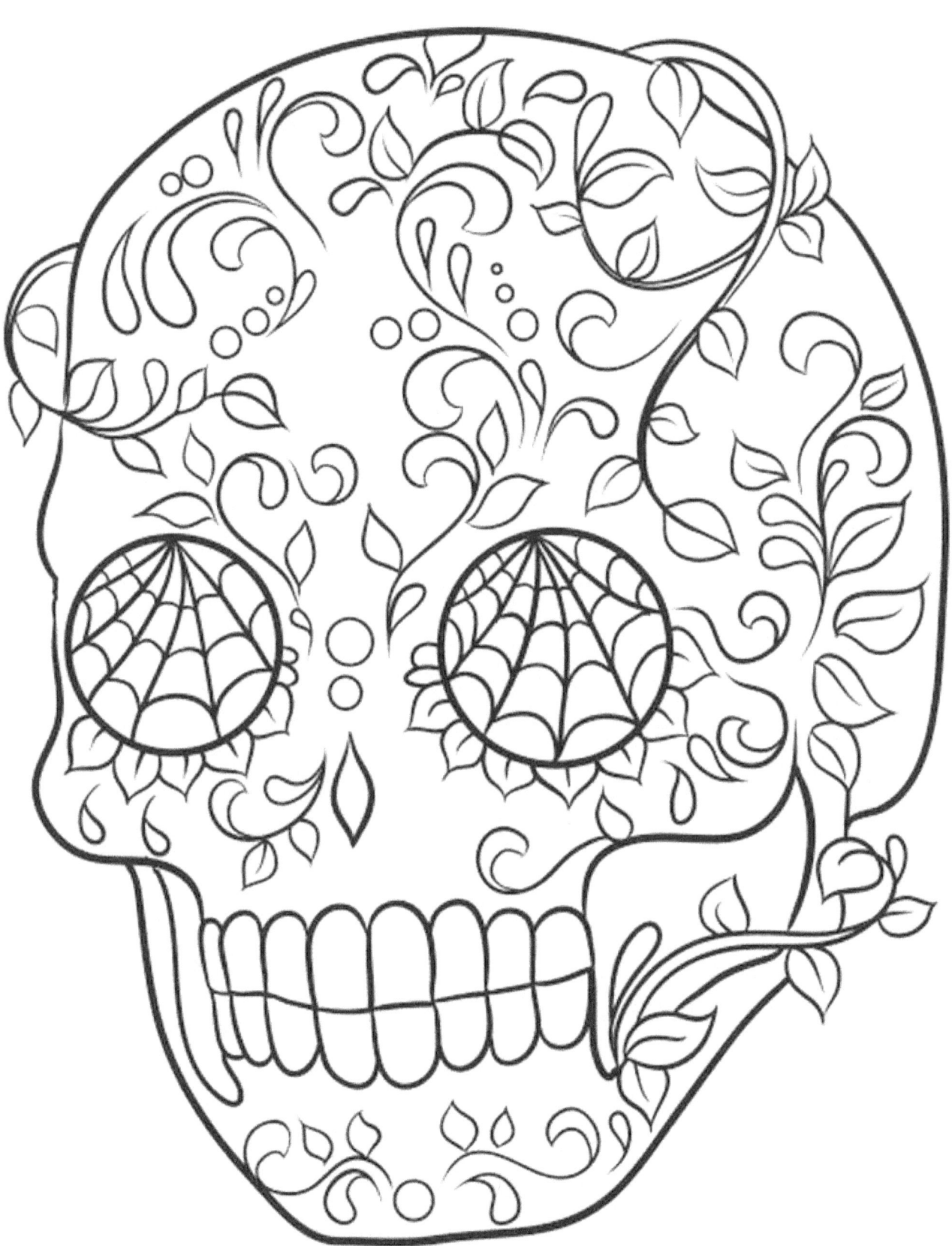

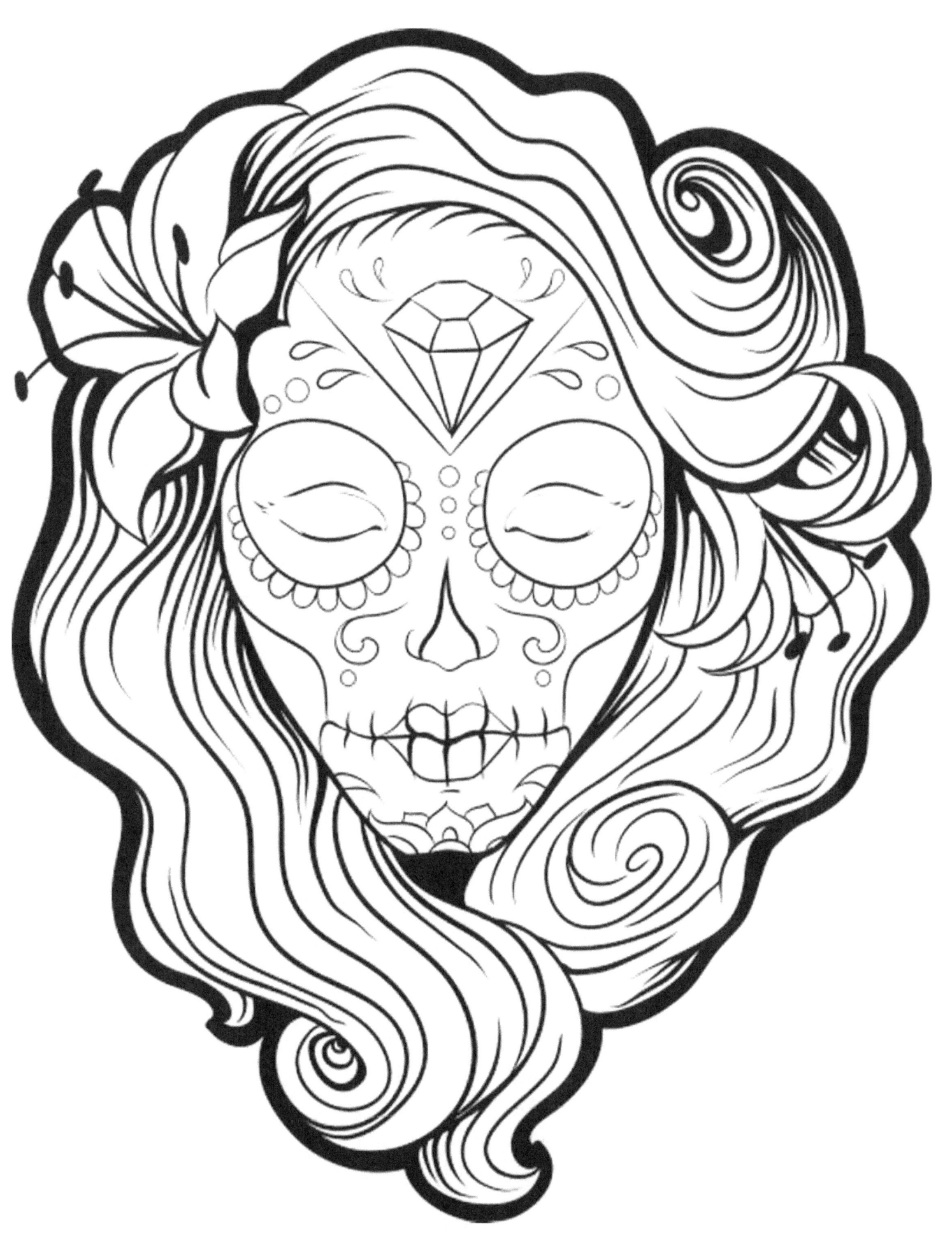

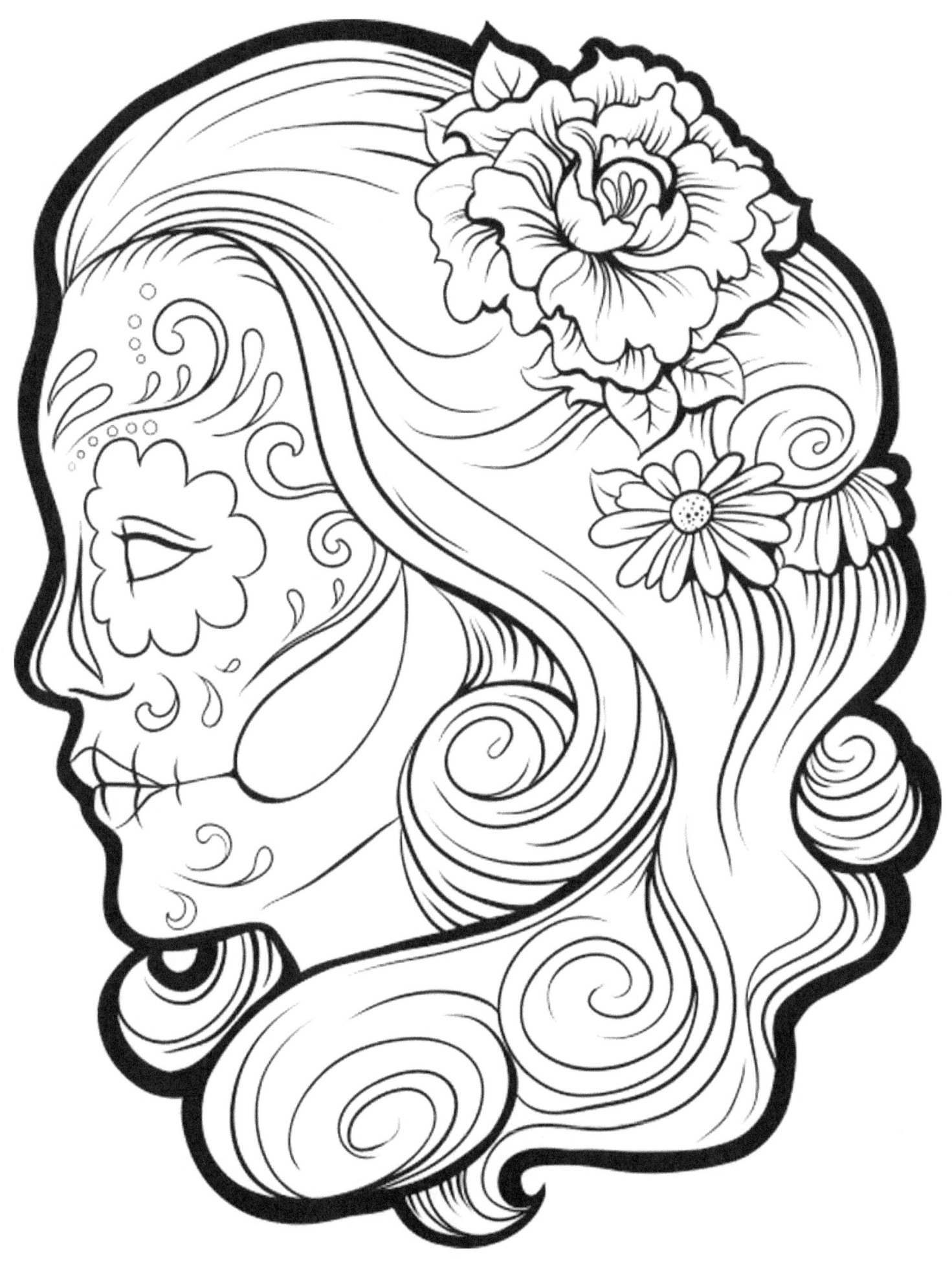

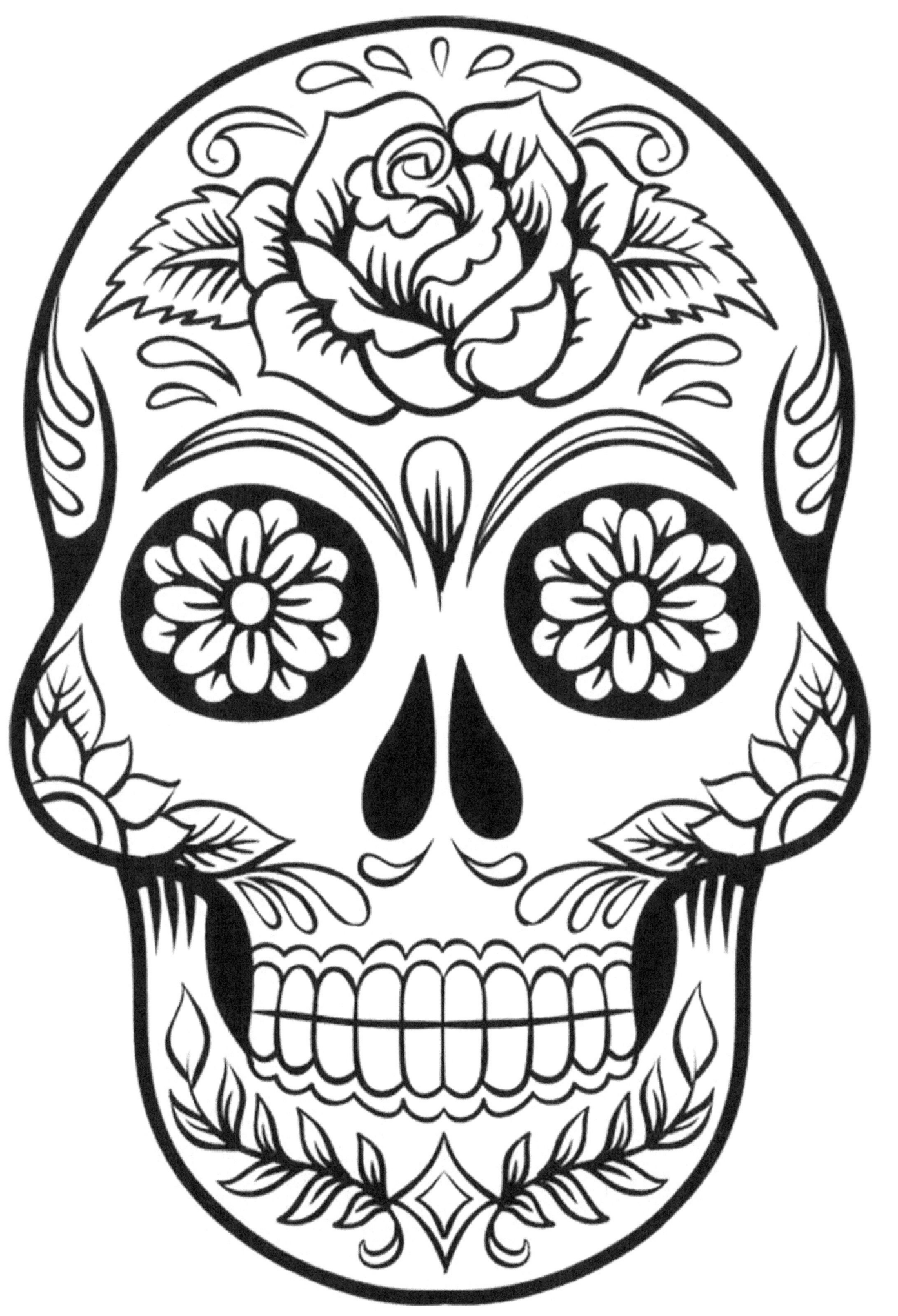

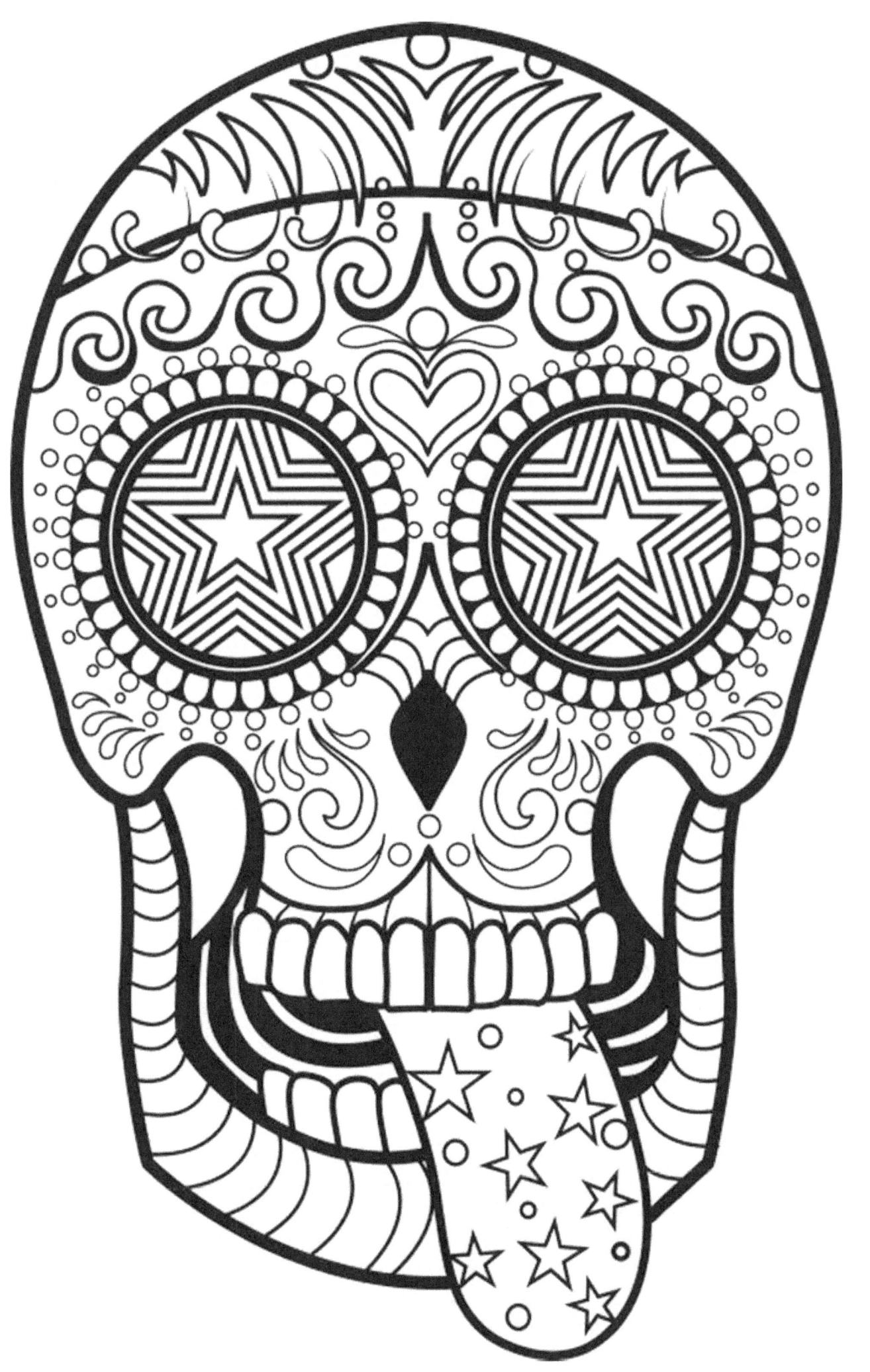

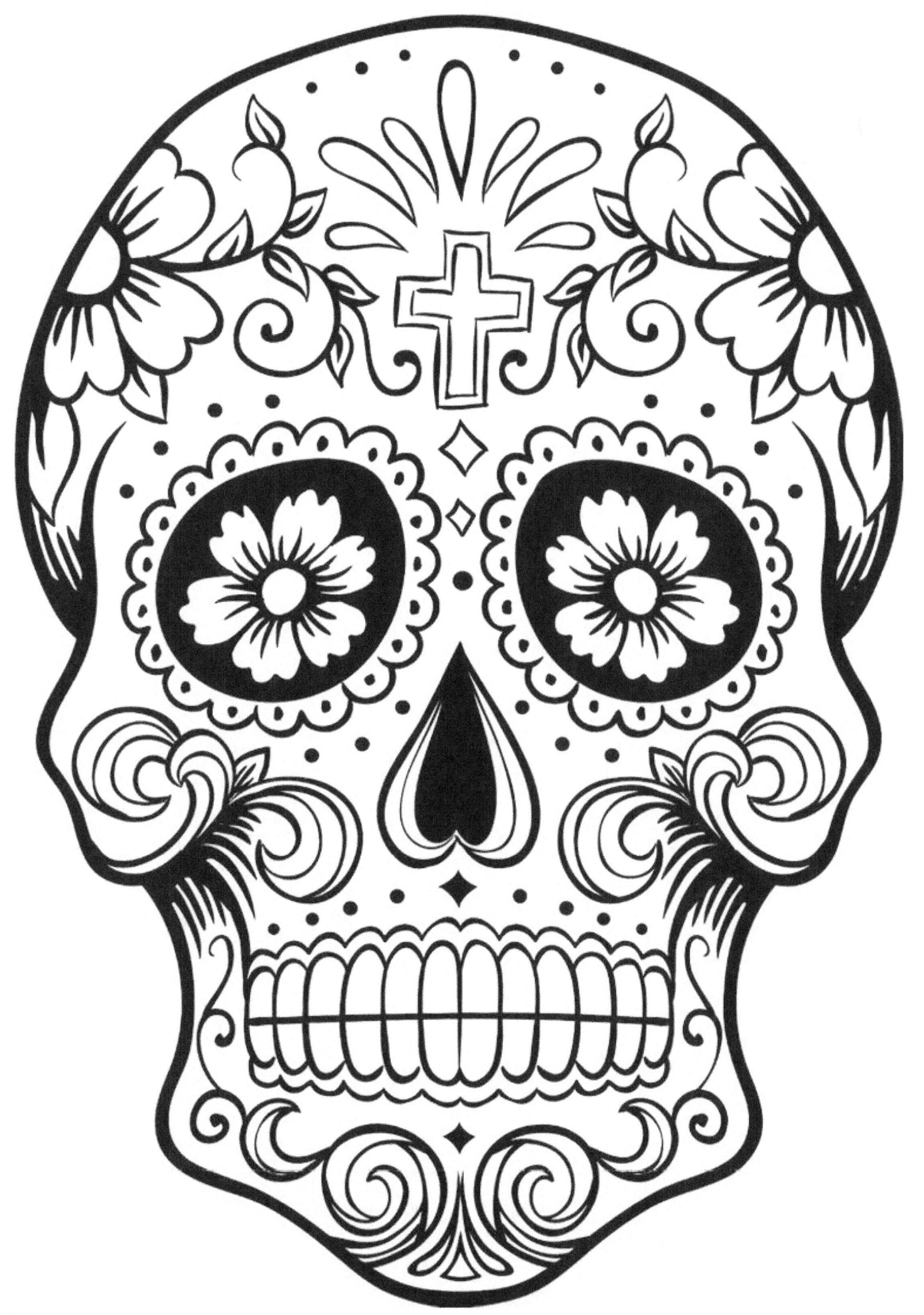

www.ingramcontent.com/pod-product-compliance
Lightning Source LLC
Chambersburg PA
CBHW082025230526
45466CB00023B/3372